PRODUCTION REPORT NO. 1: HEALTH PROBLEMS. THERE HAVE BEEN THREE OR FOUR CRISES SO FAR. THE WORST WAS LOWER BACK PAIN THAT BOTHERED ME FOR SIX MONTHS STARTING IN JANUARY '91. WHEN IT GOT BAD, I COULDN'T EVEN SIT AT MY DESK, AND I HAD TO DRAW LYING IN BED. MORE RECENTLY, I GOT THE FLU WHILE WORKING ON THE COLOR EPISODE WHERE WE ANNOUNCED THE POPULARITY CONTEST RESULTS (IN VOL. 7). I WAS SO DIZZY AND NAUSEOUS, AND I PRACTICALLY DID THE EPISODE ON AUTOPILOT. RIGHT NOW, I SEEM PHYSICALLY HEALTHY, BUT MY BRAIN STILL SUFFERS FROM CHRONIC INSANITY.

—YOSHIHIRO TOGASHI, 1991

Born in 1966, Yoshihiro Togashi won the prestigious Tezuka Award for new manga artists at the age of 20. He debuted in Japan's WEEKLY SHONEN JUMP magazine in 1988 with the romantic comedy manga **Tende Showaru Cupid**. His hit comic **YuYu Hakusho** ran in WEEKLY SHONEN JUMP from 1990 to 1994. Togashi's other manga include **I'm Not Afraid of Wolves!**, **Level E**, and **Hunter x Hunter**.

YUYU HAKUSHO VOL. 6
The SHONEN JUMP Graphic Novel Edition

This graphic novel contains material that was originally published in English in **SHONEN JUMP** #22-26.

STORY AND ART BY
YOSHIHIRO TOGASHI

English Adaptation/Gary Leach
Translation/Lillian Olsen
Touch-Up Art & Lettering/Kathryn Renta
Graphics & Cover Design/Sean Lee
Interior Design/Courtney Utt
Editors/Shaenon K. Garrity & Michelle Pangilinan

Managing Editor/Elizabeth Kawasaki
Director of Production/Noboru Watanabe
Editorial Director/Alvin Lu
Executive Vice President & Editor in Chief/Hyoe Narita
Sr. Director of Licensing & Acquisitions/Rika Inouye
Vice President of Sales & Marketing/Liza Coppola
Vice President of Strategic Development/Yumi Hoashi
Publisher/Seiji Horibuchi

Printed in the U.S.A.

Published by VIZ, LLC
P.O. Box 77010 • San Francisco, CA 94107

SHONEN JUMP Graphic Novel Edition
10 9 8 7 6 5 4 3 2 1
First printing, January 2005

SHONEN JUMP GRAPHIC NOVEL

YuYu HAKUSHO™

Vol.6
The Dark Tournament

STORY AND ART BY
YOSHIHIRO TOGASHI

THE STORY SO FAR:
うらめしあつこ
浦飯温子
Atsuko Urameshi
Yusuke's mother. Only 29 years old (still young!).
うらめしゆうすけ
浦飯幽助
Yusuke Urameshi
The protagonist. Eighth grade in Sarayashiki Public Jr. High. Used to be a delinquent to the core.
ゆきむらけいこ
雪村螢子
Keiko Yukimura
Yusuke's childhood friend. As you can see, she's quite cute.
くわばら
桑原
Kuwabara
Yusuke's eternal rival. Has a strong sixth sense that belies his [ugly] face.

Botan
Guide to the Underworld.
Yusuke's guardian of sorts.

Yukina
Belongs to a family of
demons called Ice Maidens.

This is the story of hapless Yusuke Urameshi, who got into a car accident trying to save a kid, and became a ghost. He's come back to life after the Underworld's King Enma gave him a number of ordeals. He's now an Underworld Detective that tracks down the most notorious demons.

Now that Yusuke and friends have defeated the Four Beasts, the rest of the demons have realized that they are a formidable team. But with success comes peril, as they have also become the targets of demons out for fame and fortune. What will happen next…?

YU YU HAKUSHO VOLUME 6 THE DARK TOURNAMENT

CONTENTS

SPRINGTIME FOR KUWABARA!!

I HAVEN'T WATCHED IT YET, THOUGH. HONEST.
IT'S MY NEXT UNDERWORLD ASSIGNMENT.
UNDER-WORLD? WHAT'S THAT?
PROMISE ME, YUSUKE, THAT... WHENEVER POSSIBLE, I'LL BE THE FIRST TO KNOW!
.....
I... I THOUGHT...
...BOTAN TOLD YOU ALL ABOUT IT!
RIGHT.
SHE SAID YOU'RE WORKING FOR A PRIVATE DETECTIVE.
OH, I SEE. "UNDERWORLD" IS THE NAME OF HIS AGENCY!
MASTER OF DECEPTION!
HEY, BOTAN!!
KUWABARA'S HOUSE

YUSUKE'S DECIDED TO GET SERIOUS ABOUT HIS CAREER OPTIONS, SO HE'S TAKEN A JOB AS A DETECTIVE'S ASSISTANT. HE WAS INVESTIGATING A DRUG RING WHEN A DESERTER TOOK REFUGE IN THE SCHOOL. THE RINGLEADERS SENT AN ASSASSIN TRAINED IN HYPNOTISM, AND HE HYPNOTIZED THE TEACHERS TO ACT LIKE A MOVIE ZOMBIE MOB AS A DISTRACTION WHILE HE DEALT WITH THE DESERTER. THE TEACHERS, LEFT UNGUIDED, GOT A LITTLE OUT OF HAND UNTIL THE HYPNOTIC EFFECTS WORE OFF.
WHAT'S ALL THIS GARBAGE?!
NOW, NOW...
...I WAS TRYING TO EXPLAIN STUFF TO KEIKO WITHOUT GIVING TOO MUCH AWAY.
THIS IS THE "EXPLANATION" I MANAGED TO COOK UP, AND SHE SEEMED TO BUY IT. NOT BAD, EH?
FOR LAME IMPROV COMEDY, MAYBE.
AS YOU KNOW, WE MUST BE DISCREET!
THE FACTS ABOUT YOUR JOB ARE TOP SECRET.
IT'S TOO DANGEROUS FOR KEIKO TO KNOW OF THE UNDERWORLD.
HMM... CAN'T ARGUE THAT.
BOTAN'S CAT FACE. QUITE DISTRACTING.
HEY, HOW 'BOUT WE WATCH THIS THING?
I'M ACHIN' TO KNOW WHAT'S ON IT.
WHY? IT HAS NOTHING TO DO WITH YOU THIS TIME.
WHAT-EVER.
CLICK
ZZSHHH
WHOA...

SPRINGTIME FOR KUWABARA!!

YOUR MISSION THIS TIME...
...IS SIMPLICITY ITSELF: A RESCUE!
THE RESCUEE: A NON-HUMAN GIRL.
THAT ISN'T TO SAY SHE'S ENTIRELY IN-HUMAN, BUT ANYWAY...
...SHE'S BEING HELD IN A MANSION IN BONE ULCER VILLAGE, A VERY DESOLATE PLACE.
THIS MUCH WE'VE LEARNED FROM RELIABLE UNDERWORLD MESSENGER BIRDS.
SHE'S AN ICE MAIDEN, BELONGING TO THE DEMONIC FAMILY OF WINTER SPIRITS. THEY ARE NOTED FOR THE BEAUTIFUL JEWELS THEY PRODUCE...
SHE'S BEEN TAKEN BY A HEARTLESS HUMAN WHO IS FORCING HER TO PRODUCE THESE JEWELS...
.....
SHE DOES SO THROUGH...
KOENMA'S EYE

...HER TEARS.
THEY MUST BE PURE RARE CRYSTAL!
WORTH HUNDREDS OF MILLIONS ON THE BLACK MARKET!
SO THIS DUDE IS MAKING HER CRY TO GET THESE JEWELS?
YES. THE PERPETRATOR IS A HUMAN GEM DEALER NAMED GONZO TARUKANE.
HE'S ALWAYS EARNED HIS LIVING BY UNSCRUPULOUS MEANS, BUT THE ICE MAIDEN'S JEWELS HAVE MADE HIM ENORMOUSLY RICH AND POWERFUL.
WHY DO I DRAW SUCH PUG-UGLIES?
YEESH! HE SURE LOOKS LIKE A SLEAZE!
WORSE THAN ANY DEMON!
ESST
AND THIS IS AN IMAGE OF THE GIRL...
...TELEPATHICALLY RELAYED BY THE BIRDS.
ポテト王子

SHE'S CONFINED TO A ROOM AT TARUKANE'S SUMMER MANSION.
THE BARRIER OF TALISMANS MUST KEEP HER RESTRAINED.

HUH?
I'M IN LOVE...
QUIVER
QUIVER
YI!
LET'S GO TO THAT VILLAGE!
WHAT? NOW?
OF COURSE NOW!!
SHIZURU, LEND ME ENOUGH TO GET TO BONE ULCER!
HONETADARE VILLAGE? THAT'S WAY IN THE NEXT PRE-FECTURE.
DUHH
BUT WE HAVEN'T EVEN FINISHED THE VIDEO.
WHAT MORE DO WE NEED TO KNOW? SHE'S SUFFERING! AND WE KNOW WHY!
STOMP
STOMP
HUSTLE YER BUTT, OR I'LL GO WITHOUT YOU!!
WHAT'S GOT HIM FIRED UP?
MY IDIOT BROTHER'S ON ANOTHER TEAR. YOU GUYS TAKING OFF TOO?
I'M STAYING FOR TEA.
UH...
WHAT IS GOING ON?
MMM...
SPRING-TIME FOR KUWABARA.

TARUKANE ESTATE...
VVROOM
SCREEK
WE'VE BEEN WAITING FOR YOU, SIR.
HOW'S YUKINA? HAS SHE SHED ANY TEARS?
NOT RECENTLY. HER EMOTIONS...
...HAVE RATHER FLATTENED OUT OF LATE.
HMPH. SILLY FREAK... SHE'S BECOME INDIFFERENT TO MY NEEDS.
I'VE BROUGHT SPECIALISTS TO... REKINDLE HER INTEREST.
AND THEY ARE...
GLANCE
TOMP TOOM

THE TOGURO BROTHERS...
...BROKERS OF DARKNESS!
BROKERS OF DARKNESS?
GOOD GOLLY MISS MOLLY!
DEMONS IN THE BUSINESS OF PROVIDING MONSTERS!!
FOR EVERY-THING FROM SIDESHOWS TO ASSAULT FORCES.
THEY KNOW HOW TO DEAL WITH FREAKS.
SET A THIEF TO CATCH A THIEF, THEY SAY...
LEAVE IT TO US.

HEH HEH...
TWEET
TWEET
TWEET
CHIRP
I ENVY YOU.
YOU CAN FLY FROM HERE.
PEEP?
ZAK
AS FOR ME...
!
TAK
TAK
I AM TRAPPED... BY SUBTLE BUT EFFECTIVE RESTRAINTS.
GO!
FWAP
FWAP
FWAP
FWAP

WHOOOOO
HM?
HEH... THE FREAK KNOWS WE'RE HERE.
THIS BLAST OF COLD AIR IS A WARNING, LIKE A RATTLESNAKE SOUNDING OFF.
WON'T DO HER ANY GOOD, THOUGH.
WITHIN THIS CAGE, SHE HAS NO BITE.
CREEAK
THERE SHE IS...
...AS EXPRESSIVE AS A GLACIER.

DRIP...
SLASH!
SHE WON'T CRY, SCREAM, OR TWITCH AN EYEBROW ANYMORE!
THAT WON'T WORK. FOR FIVE YEARS NOW, SHE'S RESISTED ALL **PHYSICAL** COERCION.
STAY AWAY!!
!
OH...!
FWAP
FWAP
FWAP
FWAP
GO!
HEH.

PEEP!!
!!
HEE HEE HEE.
PEEP!
PEEP!
DASH
HOLD HER.
DON'T HURT THEM!!
NO... PLEASE...!!
SQUEEZE
CHEEP... CHEE!
STAB
CHEE...!
SO THESE LITTLE FRIENDS OF YOURS HELP GET YOU THROUGH YOUR LONELY DAYS...
...EH, LITTLE GIRL?

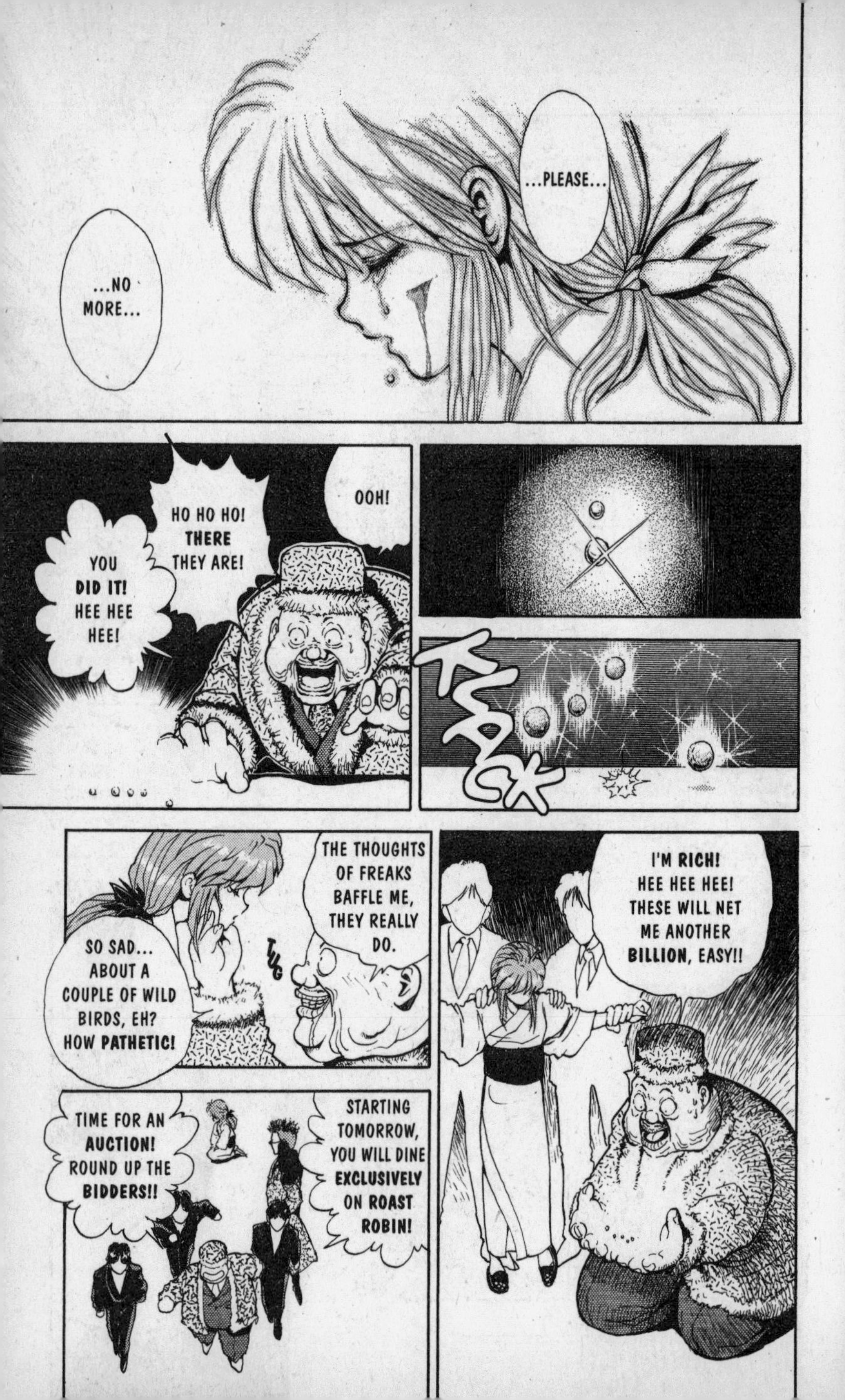

...PLEASE...
...NO MORE...
OOH!
HO HO HO! THERE THEY ARE!
YOU DID IT! HEE HEE HEE!
I'M RICH! HEE HEE HEE! THESE WILL NET ME ANOTHER BILLION, EASY!!
THE THOUGHTS OF FREAKS BAFFLE ME, THEY REALLY DO.
TUG
SO SAD... ABOUT A COUPLE OF WILD BIRDS, EH? HOW PATHETIC!
STARTING TOMORROW, YOU WILL DINE EXCLUSIVELY ON ROAST ROBIN!
TIME FOR AN AUCTION! ROUND UP THE BIDDERS!!

MY ADVICE, LITTLE GIRL? FORGET BEING STUBBORN AND LEARN TO CRY ON DEMAND.
YOU'LL BE FREE THEN-- FREE OF MY BROTHER AND ME, AT LEAST.
SNAP
SLAM
HEE HEE! THAT SHOW WAS WORTH YOUR EXORBITANT FEE. I'LL BE CALLING ON YOUR SERVICES QUITE OFTEN.
SAKASHITA, CHECK ON HER IN A LITTLE WHILE. SEE IF SHE'S MADE ANY MORE JEWELS!
ACTUALLY, MASTER TARU-KANE...
HM?
PSST
PSST
WHAT?!

INTRU-
DERS?!
OOF.
NO DOUBT SENT BY ONE OF MY COMPETITORS, TO DISCOVER THE SECRET OF MY JEWELS.
THEY'LL HAVE A BIT OF A GAUNTLET TO RUN. THE WHOLE VILLAGE IS PRACTICALLY MY FORTRESS.
REALLY SOMETHING, REACHING MOUNTAINS AFTER ONLY AN HOUR BY TRAIN AND BUS.
THERE'S PLENTY OF COUNTRYSIDE OUTSIDE THE CITY, BUT ONLY THE RICH GET TO ENJOY IT MUCH.
THESE TIRE TRACKS OUGHT TO LEAD US TO THE MANSION.
I ALREADY HAVE MEN PLACED ON SECURITY DUTY.
THEY WON'T GET ANYWHERE NEAR HERE...

PATIENCE, LADY OF THE SNOW!!
I'LL SAVE YOU! SO I SWEAR!!
WOOOOW
WOW! SHE REALLY GOT TO HIM!
GOOD THING HE DIDN'T SEE THE REST OF THE VIDEO.
ONE MORE THING, YUSUKE, AND THIS IS IMPORTANT...
...AS IT INVOLVES A PERSONAL DEBT YOU OWE.
THE GIRL'S NAME IS YUKINA...
...AND SHE IS HIEI'S SISTER.
!!
SHOOF

BUZZ OFF, GUYS.
THIS IS PRIVATE PROPERTY.
IT'S LATE, WE MISSED OUR TRAIN, AND WE THOUGHT...
...WE COULD STAY THE NIGHT AT TARUKANE'S MANSION!!
NO CHANCE OF THAT.
RRRIP
OH WELL...
HIS LEG...
?!
GACK!!!
SORRY, BUT YOU'LL HAVE TO LEAVE...
...IN BODY BAGS.
SHLOORP
SHLOORP

⑩ With a pencil, blacken out the Hit Point boxes for the amount of damage that you receive. You'll be KO'ed once the bar gets full! Refer to p.68 for how to play.

SPLOCK
ONCE I SEND YOU TO THE AFTERLIFE...
SPLORTCH
...YOU MAY PONDER YOUR FOLLY IN SETTING FOOT ON THE PROPERTY OF GONZO TARU-KANE.
NO HUMAN WHO SEES ME LIKE THIS LIVES TO TELL OF IT!
DON'T THINK OF TURNING BACK.
THAT'S GROSS, EVEN FOR A DEMON!!
EEEEWW
.....

THE BLACK BOOK CLUB!!

READ THIS WAY

WHOOSH
HAH! ALL HIGH AND MIGHTY, ARE WE?!

GEH—
GUH—
ZAAAM

!!
WHADDAYA KNOW...
SOMETHING WRONG?
HIRUE'S AURA JUST WENT PFFT.
THE INTRUDERS GOT HIM, I THINK.
WHAT?!
ARE YOUR MEN THAT WEAK?!
YOU TOLD ME YOU COULD HANDLE ANYTHING!
I'VE PAID GOOD MONEY FOR YOU TO DO JUST THAT— NO LESS!!
NO. THIS TELLS ME WE AREN'T DEALING WITH...
...JUST ANY RATS OFF THE STREET.
PROVE IT!
AND WE WILL.

HOW, EXACTLY?
HMMM...
LET ME SEE WHAT YOU CAN DO.
SAKASHITA! TRIPLE THE SECURITY OUTSIDE!
COME, I'LL SHOW YOU SOME-THING.
KRRR KRR
NICE FREAK MENA-GERIE...
MY MOST PRIZED ACQUISI-TIONS.
THEY'VE COST ME A BUNDLE, BUT THEY'RE WORTH IT.
BEHOLD!
GARR...

THE ELDER TOGURO WILL SIT THIS ONE OUT.

JUST BY LOOKING AT ME...
...YOU WOULDN'T THINK I LOVED ANIMALS.
GRONK
GRONK
YOU IDIOT! GET BACK OUT HERE! WHO'S GOING TO GUARD YUKINA IF YOU DIE?!
I CAN'T CALL HER OFF! SHE DOESN'T HAVE THE BRAIN CAPACITY TO TAKE COMMANDS!!
MM... TOO BAD.
30% SHOULD BE ENOUGH...
RUURRR
...TO BEAT THIS POOR BEAST.

CRACKLE
HAAAH!
CRACKLE
WOW!
HIS MUSCLES ARE EXPANDING!!
I RATHER LACK USEFUL SKILLS.
CHANGING MUSCLE MASS... THAT'S ABOUT IT.
GRRAUGH!

CROOOMP
?!
CLUTCH
GONNA COST A BIT TO REPAIR THIS FLOOR.
WELL, SWEETIE... I'M SORRY, BUT YOUR MASTER INSISTS...
...ON A DEMONSTRATION.

OOOH...

TWITCH
TWITCH
PHEW. THE CLIENT MAY HAVE ORDERED IT...
...BUT I'M NOT HAPPY DOING IT.
HEH...
HA HA...
HA HA HA HA!
THAT'S SPLENDID! SIMPLY SPLENDID!!
I'LL DOUBLE YOUR FEE! TRIPLE IT!
YOU'LL BE MY PERSONAL BODYGUARD!!
I'LL THINK ABOUT IT.
BY THE WAY, WHEN YOU SAID 30%, DID YOU MEAN...
...YOU BEAT HELEN WITH ONLY A THIRD OF YOUR STRENGTH?!
THAT'S 'BOUT IT.
20% PROBABLY WOULD HAVE DONE...
...BUT I'M A TIMID GUY AT HEART.
SAKA-SHITA!! GET ON THE PHONE!
THE AUCTION IS ALL SET, SIR...
IT'S NOT ABOUT THE AUCTION!
NO PARKING!
I WANT YOU TO CALL THE BLACK BOOK CLUB!!

THIS IS A FABULOUS OPPORTUNITY TO SQUEEZE SOME LOOT OUT OF THE FIVE AT THE BBC!
YES! WHY SHOULD I WATCH SUCH AN EYE-CATCHING, MONEY-MAKING SHOW BY MYSELF?!
YOU WISH TO MAKE THINGS MORE... INTERESTING.
!
HEH...
HEE HEE... YUKINA'S TEARS OF ICE ARE NOT JUST ENCHANTED JEWELS, BUT VERITABLE MONEY MAGNETS!!
I'LL RAKE IN MORE BILLIONS IF I MANIPULATE THE ODDS, AND WITH THE PAY-PER-VIEW REVENUE...
PINKY FINGER, NOT THUMB
HEH HEH... IT MAY BE AS YOU SAY, MY FRIEND.
BUT I'LL ENJOY MYSELF TO THE FULLEST UNTIL THEN!
I DON'T FORESEE YOU MEETING A PLEASANT END.
......

READ THIS WAY

WOULDN'T MISS IT FOR THE WORLD.
TRUE ENOUGH. I COULD USE A FRESH DIVERSION.
THE USUAL HOBBIES ARE BECOMING... TEDIOUS.
BUT THERE IS ALWAYS AMUSEMENT IN OTHER PEOPLE'S MISFORTUNES.
HA HA HA
SO...
...WHAT'S ON THE CARD TODAY?
I HAVE TWO INTRUDERS ON MY ESTATE WHO APPEAR TO BE AFTER THE SECRET OF MY TEARS OF ICE.
I'D LIKE US TO WAGER ON HOW THEY'LL DO AGAINST THE BROKERS OF DARKNESS.
HMM... YOU'RE NOT SAYING WHO THESE INTRU-DERS ARE.
STILL, YOU'VE MANAGED TO INTRIGUE US.
HEE HEE... I KNEW I WOULD.
EXCELLENT. ALWAYS NICE TO SPREAD THE WEALTH AROUND.
HERE'S THE SITUATION, GENTLEMEN-- THE INTRUDERS ARE FOLLOWING THIS ROAD...
...WHILE THE BROKERS STATIONED OUTSIDE ARE CONVERGING TO INTERCEPT.
TARUKANE MANSION

I HAVE 12 MEN OUTSIDE, AND THREE IN THE MANSION.
EACH IS CAPABLE OF WIPING OUT A SQUAD OF ARMY SPECIAL FORCES.
AH, I SEE... THE BETTING IS JUST TO SPICE THINGS UP.
YOU'RE REALLY OUT TO FLEECE US FOR THE PRIVILEGE OF WATCHING THE SLAUGHTER!!
EVER THE BUSINESSMAN.
.....
SHALL WE BEGIN?
THE EVENT IS TWO INTRUDERS VS. THE 12 BROKERS OUTSIDE.
THIS WILL PAY OUT TWICE THE AMOUNT ANTED BY THE WINNER.
200 MILLION YEN ON THE BROKERS!
SAME HERE— 200 MILLION.
I BET 250 MILLION ON THE BROKERS!!
HEE HEE... THEY FELL FOR IT. THE REPUTATION OF THE BROKERS IS QUITE PERSUASIVE...
HEH
I'VE HEARD THAT RANDO AND SUZAKU, DEMONS OF CONSIDERABLE STATURE, WERE RECENTLY TAKEN DOWN BY TWO HUMAN BOYS. IF THESE ARE THE INTRUDERS, OUR GUYS MAY BE FACING MORE THAN THEY CAN HANDLE.

GASP!
I BET FIVE BILLION... ON THE INTRUDERS!!
RUMOR HAS IT TWO HUMAN BOYS HAVE BEEN GOING AROUND STAMPING OUT DEMONS.
BECAUSE THERE ARE TWO OF THEM.
HOW CAN ANY SANE PERSON EXPECT TWO HUMANS TO BEAT A DOZEN DEMONS?
MUTTER MUTTER
ARE YOU CRAZY?!
!
NERTS!! TRUST THAT SHREWD PUNK TO KEEP HIS EAR TO THE GROUND!!
HA HA... YOUNG SAKYO, ALWAYS THE GAMBLER.
SIX MORE OF MY MEN HAVE GONE THE WAY OF THE FIRST.
THESE HUMANS ARE GOOD.
WHAT NOW?!
MM...!!

SIX DOWN!!
YOU GOT LUCKY, HUMAN SCUM!!
WE'RE READY FOR YOU NOW!!
CLASSIC REDSHIRTS...
STUFF IT, YOU PUG-UGLIES!
OUTTA MY WAY! I'M BURNIN' WITH ROMANTIC FURY!!
HE'S CRANKED TO 11!

SHWAASH
YOU ASKED FOR IT! HEE-YAH!!
BBOOMM!

NEXT?!!
DA-DUM
SIX MORE, IN UNDER SIX SECONDS...
.....
SAKASHITA, PREPARE SAKYO'S PAYMENT.
UH...
...YESSIR.
THAT'S 10 **BILLION** FOR ME. NICE...
SO MUCH FOR THAT.

NEXT UP: THE OGRE TRIAD!!

THAT MUST BE THE MANSION.
.....
WHERE MY HEART'S DESIRE IS CAGED.
I'M HERE, SNOWGIRL!! I'LL SAVE YOU!!
YOU MIGHT WANT TO CONFIRM THAT SHE'S HERE.
WONDER WHAT HE'D THINK IF HE KNEW HIS "SNOW-GIRL" IS HIEI'S SISTER?
RIGHT. HMM... I DON'T PICK UP ANYTHING.
THOSE TALISMANS WE SAW IN THE VIDEO MUST SHIELD AGAINST MY SIXTH SENSE.
ON THE OTHER HAND, I'M PICKING UP THREE DEMONIC AURAS WAY STRONGER THAN THE DOZEN WE JUST WIPED OUT...

THREE DEMONS LEFT, EH? WELL, THEY MAY BE POWERFUL, BUT I'M READY TO TAKE ON ANYTHING.
I'VE GOT MY REIGUN RAPID-FIRE DOWN TO A SWEET SCIENCE.
AND ME...
...I FELT NEW POWER SURGING WITHIN ME AS SOON AS I RECOVERED FROM MY LAST INJURIES.
WE'VE GONE UP A LEVEL!!
LET'S GO!!

...MR. TARUKANE.
LET US PROCEED...
AH, BUT OUR NEXT CONTENDERS ARE A DIFFERENT MATTER.
...THAT THERE ARE HUMANS ABLE TO DEFEAT BROKERS OF DARKNESS, IF ONLY THE UNDERLINGS.
INTERESTING, THOUGH...
SNAP
THE OGRE TRIAD!!

VERTEX ONE: MIYU-KI.
VERTEX TWO: INMA-KI.
VERTEX THREE: GOKUMON-KI.
YOU'VE CLEARLY INVESTED HEAVILY IN THIS SPECTACLE, MR. TARUKANE.
THESE THREE ARE TOP-LEVEL DEMONS!!
THE SECRET OF THE TEARS OF ICE IS WORTH IT, EH?
EXACTLY. SO, THE SECOND EVENT IS THE INTRUDERS VS. THE OGRE TRIAD.
PLACE YOUR BETS.
PAYOUT IS THREE TIMES THE AMOUNT ANTED.
I'M PUTTING 500 MILLION ON THE BROKERS!!
500 MILLION ON THE BROKERS FOR ME!!
300 MILLION ON THE TRIAD!!
PUFF

TWENTY BILLION... ON THE INTRUDERS!!
DOOM
WHAT...?
URK
......
THAT'S NOT A VOTE OF CONFI-DENCE.
EASY ENOUGH TO REMEDY. WIN!!
AS YOU WISH...
BLAM
BLAM

BLAST! THEY'RE FAST!
KEEP FIRING!!
?!
TZING
TZING
TWUP
TWUP
GUNS ARE USELESS AGAINST THEM!
CRINGE!
TH-THEY'RE NOT HUMAN!!
IT'S OBVIOUS WHEN AND WHERE YOU'RE GOING TO SHOOT.
QUANTITY CAN'T REPLACE QUALITY, DUDES.
STEP ASIDE.
PRE-CISELY.

HELLO. I'M MIYUKI, OGRE TRIAD VERTEX ONE.
YIPES!!
BASH
HAAH!!!
CHIVALRY ON YOUR PART DOESN'T MEAN MERCY ON MY PART.
THAT'S SWEET... BUT A MISTAKE.
I CAN'T FIGHT A GIRL!
SHE'S A GIRL!!
MAN OR WOMAN, YOUNG OR OLD... YOU WANT A FIGHT, I'LL GIVE YOU ONE.
I DON'T CARE.
CHIVALRY? NEVER HEARD OF IT.
DOOM

BETTER MAKE SURE, FIRST...
SHFF
HAAH!!
DASH
!!
Y-YOU IMPERTINENT WHELP!
SILENCE!!
ARR!
RUDE, I KNOW!
BUT THAT SHOULD GIVE YOU AN IDEA OF WHAT YOU'RE UP AGAINST.
?

TODAY
FRESH
EVIL
PURE
THUMP
YOU REALLY DON'T CARE, DO YOU?
WELL, I WAS MAYBE GONNA GO A LITTLE EASY ON A REAL GIRL...
...BUT THEN I CHECKED!
"SHE'S" A DEMON CROSS-DRESSER!
NOOGA
GUH!
YOU DIDN'T!

ALONG WITH HIS OTHER TALENTS, YUSUKE'S UNPARALLELED PICKPOCKET SKILLS HAVE BEEN GREATLY ENHANCED.
MOOSH
ON THAT FIRST PASS I DISCOVERED "HER" BUST WAS EITHER AN IMPLANT OR PADDING...
...AND THAT "SHE" WAS PACKIN' MIGHTY HEAVY DOWN-STAIRS.
GAWD... CAN'T DECIDE IF I'M IMPRESSED OR GROSSED OUT!
INCREDIBLE! I DIDN'T SEE ANY OF THAT!
BIGOT! YOU BEAT ON ME BECAUSE I'M DIF-FERENT!
I'M A MAN IN BODY, BUT MY SOUL IS A WOMAN'S!!
OH, REALLY?
WHAT A LOAD!!
YOU'RE NOT A REAL CROSS-DRESSER— YOU JUST CAN'T MAKE UP YOUR MIND!
YOU MIGHT WANNA DO THAT BEFORE YOU GET INTO ANY MORE FIGHTS!!

GAAASP!!
SLUMP
YOU'RE SO RIGHT...
WHRR...
HEH
HEADS UP, TARU-KANE!!
VIP
TWO MORE, AND WE'RE IN YOUR FACE!
URK!!

READ THIS WAY

UNH!
SLASH
LOOK OUT!!
GREETINGS! I'M VERTEX TWO: INMAKI!!
HEH HEH...
FFFT
FLIP
VIP
VIP
VIP
VIP
VIP
DIDYA SEE THAT?! HIS CAPE —
— IT MADE HIM INVISIBLE!!

SLASH!!
YAAH!!
CAN YOU PINPOINT HIM?!
NO! HE'S TOO FAST! DIRECTION KEEPS SHIFTING!
CAN'T FIGHT WHAT YOU CAN'T SEE.
HEH HEH...
FLIP
CRIPES! LET'S SCRAM!!
!
NOW, URA-MESHI!!
SCOOT...
IT'S NO USE!
DASH

POWPOWBWROWPOWPOW

KA-WHAM
THEN AGAIN...
...QUANTITY CAN BE USEFUL.
H... HOW...?
SLUMP...
THAT CAPE HID YOU FROM SIGHT, BUT NOT MY SIXTH SENSE.
AN' YOU'RE NOT MUCH TO SPEAK OF ONCE YOU LOSE THE ADVANTAGE OF INVISIBILITY.
ONCE KUWABARA GAVE THE SIGNAL, I JUST FILLED THAT DOORWAY WITH REIKI BLASTS...
...SOME OF WHICH WERE BOUND TO HIT.

HEH
ONE LEFT!!
URK, AGAIN...

READ THIS WAY

DICE ROSHAMBOXING

("ROLLING FOR ROSHAMBOXING" OR JUST "ROSHAMBOXING"
--ROSHAMBO IS A FANCY NAME FOR ROCK - PAPER - SCISSORS)

1) FIRST, PLAY ROCK - PAPER - SCISSORS; THE WINNER GETS TO MAKE ONE ATTACK.
2) THE WINNER ROLLS THE DIE TO DETERMINE THE TYPE OF PUNCH.

DIE ROLL	PUNCH TYPE	ATTACK VALUE
1 2	JAB	1
3	STRAIGHT	2
4	KO PUNCH	4
5	HOOK	2
6	UPPERCUT	2

ONCE YOU KNOW THE TYPE OF PUNCH, SUBTRACT THE NUMBER OF ITS ATTACK VALUE FROM YOUR OPPONENT'S HP.

*SPECIAL RULE: A BOXER'S "BEST PUNCH" ATTACK VALUE BECOMES A 3. (FOR EXAMPLE, WHITE TIGER'S "BEST PUNCH" IS AN UPPERCUT, SO HIS UPPERCUTS ARE WORTH A 3.)

3) REPEAT STEPS (1) AND (2) THREE TIMES TO COMPLETE ONE ROUND.
(THAT MEANS IF YOU LOSE IN ROCK - PAPER - SCISSORS ALL THREE TIMES, YOU CAN'T ATTACK AT ALL IN THAT ROUND.)

4) YOUR HP WILL RECOVER BY TWO POINTS AT THE END OF EACH ROUND (IF YOU HAVEN'T BEEN KO'ED).
(IF YOUR HP BAR IS FULL, IT DOESN'T INCREASE FURTHER.)

REPEAT STEPS (1)-(4). THE ONE WHOSE HP GOES DOWN TO ZERO FIRST GETS KO'ED.

THE LAST GAMBLE!!

THAT'S THREE!!
I DIDN'T EVEN INTRODUCE MYSELF...
YOUR TIME'S RUN OUT, TARUKANE!!
THUD
I HAD NO IDEA...
...THEY'D BE THIS POWERFUL!!
THEY TOOK DOWN THE OGRE TRIAD...
...IN NO TIME FLAT!!
.....
URK!
ARR...
BLAST THOSE TWO!!

THE LAST GAMBLE!!!

PEACE, BABY!!
!
IT APPEARS I'VE WON AGAIN...
YOU'VE BEEN CLEANING UP, BUT THE REST OF US HAVE BEEN LOSING.
NOW HOLD ON THERE, MR. SAKYO.
HOW ABOUT IT, TARUKANE? GAME FOR ONE MORE ROUND?
WE'D LIKE A PIECE OF YOUR ACTION THIS TIME!!
SEVENTY BILLION IN ALL...
DUM
DAH
YOU MIGHT CONSIDER CUTTING YOUR LOSSES...
DUM
.....
DAH
DUM
I'VE SAVED THE BEST...
HEH HEH HEH...
DUM

...FOR LAST--
THE TOGURO BROTHERS VS. THE INTRUDERS!!
WHICH SHALL TRIUMPH?!
MAKE YOUR SELECTION, MR. SAKYO.
HEH HEH.
BET THE FARM ON THE INTRUDERS,
I DARE YOU.
I'LL RECOUP ALL MY LOSSES...!!
SIXTY SIX TRILLION, 200 BILLION...
...?
EH...
... WHAT?
SIXTY SIX TRILLION, 200 BILLION YEN ON THE INTRUDERS.

DOOM
SIXTY SIX TRILLION, 200 BILLION?! THAT'S THE ENTIRE JAPANESE GOVERNMENT'S BUDGET!!
YOU CAN'T BE SERIOUS!!
STAGGER...
OH, I'M QUITE SERIOUS.
IT WILL MAKE THIS CONTEST PARTICULARLY INTERESTING.
NO BACKING DOWN NOW, MR. TARUKANE.
HEH HEH HEH
HEH HEH HEH
YOU PROPOSED THESE GAMES, AND BBC RULES DICTATE YOU FINISH.
FOR OUR PART, WE'LL SIT BACK AND WATCH.
AAH... NOTHING SO AMUSING AS ANOTHER'S MISFORTUNES...
SAKYO'S INSANE!!
HUFF HUFF
HUFF HUFF
HUFF
OR... DOES HE KNOW SOMETHING ABOUT THE TEARS OF ICE? COULDN'T BE... I'VE KEPT IT AN AIRTIGHT SECRET!!

SHUUUCH
THING IS, IF I WIN, ALL THAT MONEY WILL BE MINE!! THIS WOULD BE... MY ULTIMATE GAMBLE!!
ALL RIGHT! YOU'RE ON!!
LET THE CONTEST BEGIN!!
GEEZ... FINALLY.
SAKA-SHITA! BRING YUKINA HERE.
MAKE SURE THE BBC DOESN'T FIND OUT.
WARD HER AS NECESSARY TO KEEP HER FROM RUNNING.
I DON'T DETECT ANY DEMONS!
LET'S FIND MY ICE MAIDEN AND CLEAN TARUKANE'S CLOCK!
!!

YUKINA.
'CEPT... I DON'T KNOW HER NAME!
I'LL TRY TO MAKE CONTACT!!
I WATCHED THE ENTIRE VIDEO!
HOW DO YOU KNOW?!
I SENSE SOMETHING!! NOT EVIL... IT'S HER! MUST BE!!
WHOA!!
SCREECH
PLEASE, SAY SOMETHING!!
YUKINA! CAN YOU HEAR ME?!
?
NO! GET OUT OF HERE!
KAZUMA KUWABARA, DEMON-TROUNCER. I'M HERE TO RESCUE YOU.
WHO... ARE YOU?
NO SWEAT! WE'VE ALREADY BEATEN 'EM!
NEXT, WE FREE YOU!
YOU HAVE NO CHANCE AGAINST THE BROKERS OF DARKNESS!!
YOU'RE HUMAN, AREN'T YOU?

READ THIS WAY

C'MON, TOGURO! I'M COUNTING ON YOU!!
CHECK THOSE BASTARDS ON THE MONITORS, WATCHING ALL THIS.
GUESS HE'S THE LAST OF 'EM.
.....
JUST A MATTER OF TIME!!

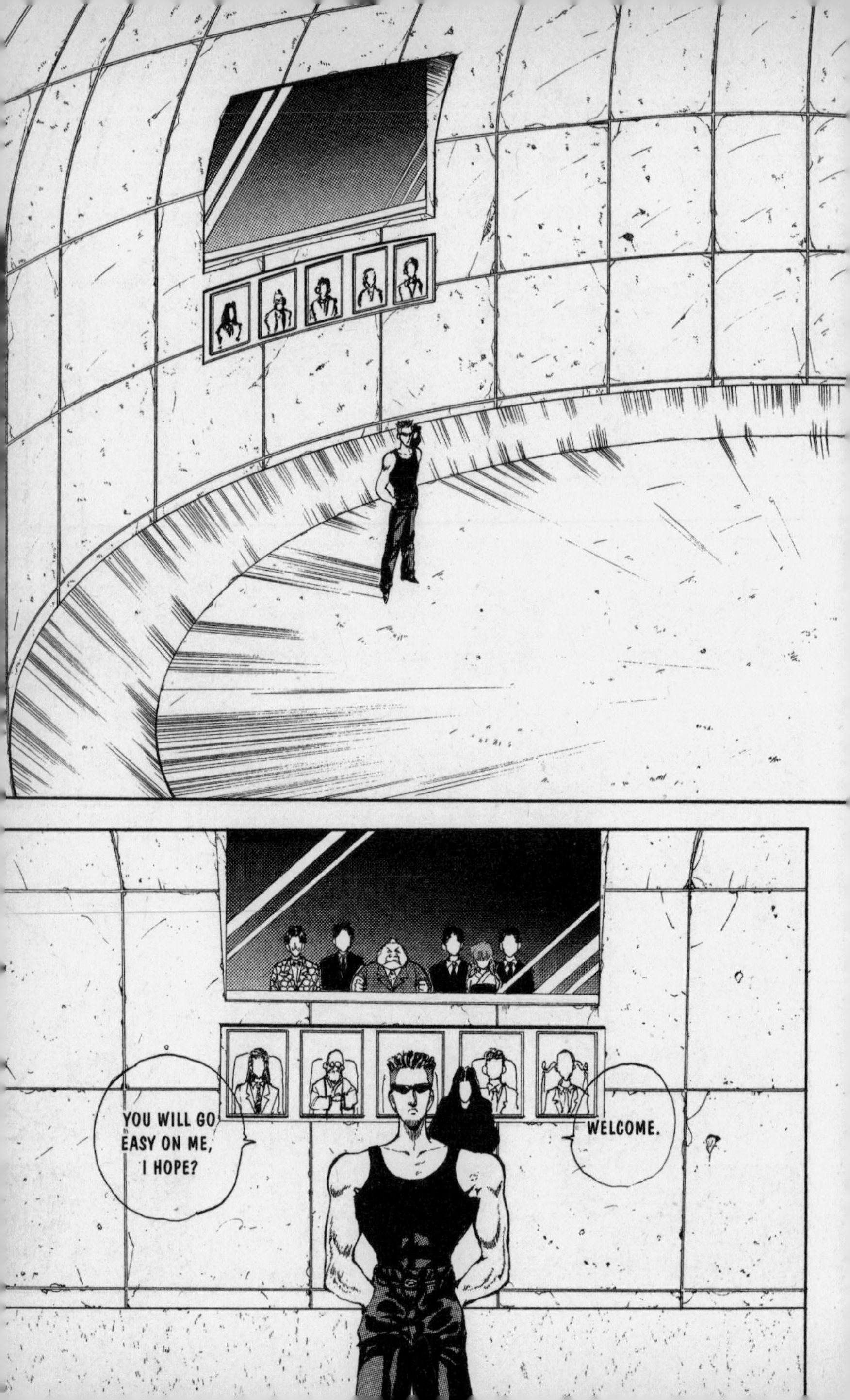
WELCOME.
YOU WILL GO EASY ON ME, I HOPE?

HEH, THE DOOF'S GOT ZILCH DEMONIC AURA. THIS'LL BE A SNAP!
.....
NO...
...YOU ASK ME, THIS GUY'S BIG TROUBLE.
WHY?
JUST A CREEPY FEELING THAT SCREAMS, "WATCH IT!"
HEH.
TUMP
CRACK
CREAK
CRACK
ULP! THAT LITTLE GUY ON HIS SHOULDER...!!
HE'S... SCRUNCHING UP?!
CRUNCH
CRACKLE

HE'S TURNED INTO A SWORD!!
AMAZING TRANSFORMATION BY MY OLDER BROTHER, DON'TCHA THINK?
ITS EFFECTIVE-NESS DEPENDS ON THE WIELDER, OF COURSE.

AS FOR ME...
HIS AURA NOW—INCREDIBLE!!
LIKE BEING HIT BY A HURRICANE!!
...I PROVIDE THE MUSCLE! LOTS OF IT!!
Y'SEE, WE'RE ONE UNIT!!

!!!
DASH

RAARR!!
WHOA! FAST!!
KRA
GRAAH!
!!
HEH.
HUUNNH...!!
!!

SLAM
KUWABARA!!
GLUH...
KOFF...
CRICK
HACK
POP
HE LEAPT BACK TO ESCAPE A FATAL IMPACT!
HE'S SMARTER THAN THAT POOR MONSTER, AT LEAST.

!!
YOUR TURN!!
HA! THAT'S FOR YOU, FREAK-O!
NAILED YOU AT POINT BLANK...

READ THIS WAY

THE FINAL BATTLE: TWO ON TWO!!
TOTTER
SKIP SKIP
THUD
GLUH!
HE'S STRONG!!
GRUH ...!!
I'M A BIT DISAP- POINTED.

READ THIS WAY
HA HA...
...HA HA HA!
HA HA, THAT'S THE TICKET!!
THIS ONE'S IN THE BAG!!
I'M GONNA WIN THE DAY!!
TOO BAD, MR. SAKYO! YOU SHOULD'VE CUT YOUR LOSSES!!
.....
I THOUGHT YOU TWO WOULD PROVIDE A BIT MORE FUN...

WHUD
WHFFT
YAH...
WHAM
EXCEL-
LENT!
DRAW IT
OUT!!
TORTURE
THOSE
PUNKS
FOR ME!
THEY HAD
THEIR FUN.
NOW THEY'LL
SUFFER...
AND DIE!

KEEP WATCHING!!
THIS IS HOW IT IS FOR ANYONE WHO TRIES TO SAVE YOU!!
LIKE LAST TIME! REMEMBER?!
NOT... GOOD...
GOING... BLACK...
BUT... WHAT...?
ARE THESE... HER THOUGHTS...?

I HEAR YOU ICE MAIDENS...
...BURN AT THE MERE TOUCH OF THESE TALISMANS.
PLEASE...
NO!
HAH!
STZZZZZ
AAI-IEE!
CRY! HA HA HA! CRY!
STZZZ
SHED TEARS! MAKE 'EM POUR!!
I'LL GET YOU OUT OF HERE ...
...SOON, I PROMISE.
.....
I HAVE A SISTER ABOUT YOUR AGE.
.....
.....

TARUKANE'S OUT OF THE COUNTRY!
SECU-RITY'S LIGHT! TODAY'S THE DAY!
WHAT ABOUT YOU? WHEN THEY DISCOVER I'M GONE...
DON'T WORRY ABOUT THAT, OKAY?
?!
THOUGHT SO. TAKE CARE OF HIM.

SO SMALL, SO FRAGILE.
SHUFF
SHUFF
I'D HOPED FOR MORE.
HURF!
IT'S HARD TO BELIEVE...
WELL, WELL...
HIS AURA'S RE-FRESHED AND GROWING.
COULD A MAN REALLY DO ALL THIS?
...TARU-KANE'S HUMAN.

STEP ASIDE, DE-MON.
YOU'RE NOT THE FIEND I'M AFTER TODAY.
THE ONE I WANT IS THE FAT, GRUBBY PIG BEHIND YOU!
YOU TALKING ABOUT ME, BOY?
YOU'VE GOT NO CHANCE!!
BUT GO AHEAD— TRY!!
TOGURO!! FINISH HIM OFF!!
HEAR THAT?
MY ORDERS. SORRY.
OUTTA MY WAY!

RAAH!
KWAP
KWAP
KWAP
AGH!
UNH!
WASTED EFFORT, KID.
I COULD PARRY YOU ALL DAY.
GRR...!!
K... KUWA-BARA...

PLAY-TIME'S OVER, TOGURO.
KILL THEM. SPLATTER THEM OVER THE WALLS.
AYE-AYE, SIR.
CRACK
CRACKLE
CRICKLE
URA-MESHI, LISTEN...
...ONE THING MIGHT WORK!!
THAT'S CRAZY!
IF WE DO THAT, YOU'RE TOAST!
I WON'T LOSE! NOT THIS WAY!!
FINE BY ME!!
PLEASE, YU-SUKE...
?

RRAAH!
TRUP
A SUICIDE CHARGE, EH?
TRUP
.....
TRUP
TRUP
PRUP
IF THAT'S HOW YOU WANT IT...
...I'LL SPLIT YOU WITH ONE STROKE!!
WHUP

HAARRRR!
!!
SHUMP

TOOK THE BLAST... RIGHT IN HIS BACK...
...BOOSTED HIM LIKE A ROCKET...
VERY... NICE...
...MOVE.

THUD
GAME OVER. SIXTY-SIX TRILLION, 270 BILLION TO ME.
BLIP
FSSSS...
BANKRUPTCY RUIN BANKRUPTCY RUIN BANKRUPTCY RUIN BANKRUPTCY!
I'LL COLLECT AT THE END OF THE MONTH.
REV UP THE HELICOPTER SAKA-SHITA!!
YUKINA AND I ARE LEAVING! NOW!
HEE HEE... WHY WORRY? WITH THE TEARS OF ICE I'LL...
TURN AROUND, FATSO.

I HEAR YOU KEPT YUKINA CAGED WITH TALISMANS.
EXPLAINS WHY MY EVIL EYE COULDN'T FIND HER.
EEP.
BUT THEN YOU LET HER OUT. CARELESS...
NO...
ST... STAY AWAY...

I WON'T KILL YOU.
YUKINA'S WORTH FAR MORE THAN YOUR PITIFUL LIFE.
WHAM
TH... THANK YOU.
UM... WHO ARE YOU?
.....
OH, JUST...
...A FRIEND OF THEIRS.
OH, MY!
THEY NEED ME!
TUP TUP TUP

STILL IN ONE PIECE?
YOU'RE A CERTIFIABLE LOONY, YOU KNOW THAT?
WELL, YOU TOLD ME YOU COULD ADJUST YOUR BLASTS.
FIGURED YOU COULD SET 'EM TO "STUN" INSTEAD OF "KILL."
YEAH, I— WHOA! ALMOST FORGOT!
WE STILL GOTTA KICK TARUKANE'S BLUBBERY BUTT!!
ARE YOU...
S'OKAY, I'M FINE.
HE COULD USE SOME ATTENTION, THOUGH.
TUPTUPTUP
UM...
Y... YUKINA?
KEEP STILL!
I CAN HEAL SOME OF THE HURT...

READ THIS WAY
I'M SO SORRY...
...YOU SUFFERED... FOR ME...
BURN MARKS! ON BOTH ARMS!
DON'T APOLOGIZE...
...TO A LOUSY HUMAN, YUKINA.
WHAT'S BEEN DONE TO YOU...
...BY ONE OF US, IS UNFORGIVABLE.
?
ALL I CAN SAY IS, WE'RE NOT ALL LIKE THAT.
HUH? HIEI?!
WE MAY NOT AMOUNT TO MUCH... BUT WE TRY, Y'KNOW?
SO, IF THAT CAN COUNT FOR ANYTHING...
MAYBE YOU WON'T HATE ALL HUMANS.
......
PLEASE ...

DON'T WORRY!
I...
...DON'T HATE HUMANS AT ALL. AND I LIKE YOU.
.....
.....
...THANK YOU...

AH, THE MEMORIES...

THE GAME I DESCRIBED ON PAGES 26 AND 68 IS ONE I INVENTED IN JUNIOR HIGH AND PLAYED AT SCHOOL WITH MY FRIENDS. WE WERE NOT ALLOWED TO BRING MANGA OR STORE-BOUGHT GAMES TO SCHOOL, AND THE TEACHERS WOULD'VE CONFISCATED THEM AND LECTURED US IF WE WERE CAUGHT. SO I CAME UP WITH MANY DIFFERENT GAMES THAT COULD EASILY BE PLAYED IN THE 10-MINUTE FREE PERIODS. I WROTE NUMBERS ON THE SIDES OF A HEXAGONAL PENCIL AND USED IT AS A DIE, AND DREW THE BOXERS IN MY NOTEBOOK. I WASN'T THE TYPE TO BLATANTLY DEFY SCHOOL REGULATIONS AND DYE MY HAIR OR WEAR THOSE BAGGY PANTS. I LIVED ONLY TO ELUDE THE LETTER OF THE LAW, AND TO COME UP WITH WAYS TO GOOF OFF WITHOUT GETTING CAUGHT BY THE TEACHERS. THERE ARE LOTS OF OTHER GAMES I MADE; I'LL PRESENT THEM IF I GET A CHANCE.

I MUST GET STRONGER!!

CRICKLE
SCRITCH SCRUNCH
SCROWNCH
......
WHEW...!
BLIP

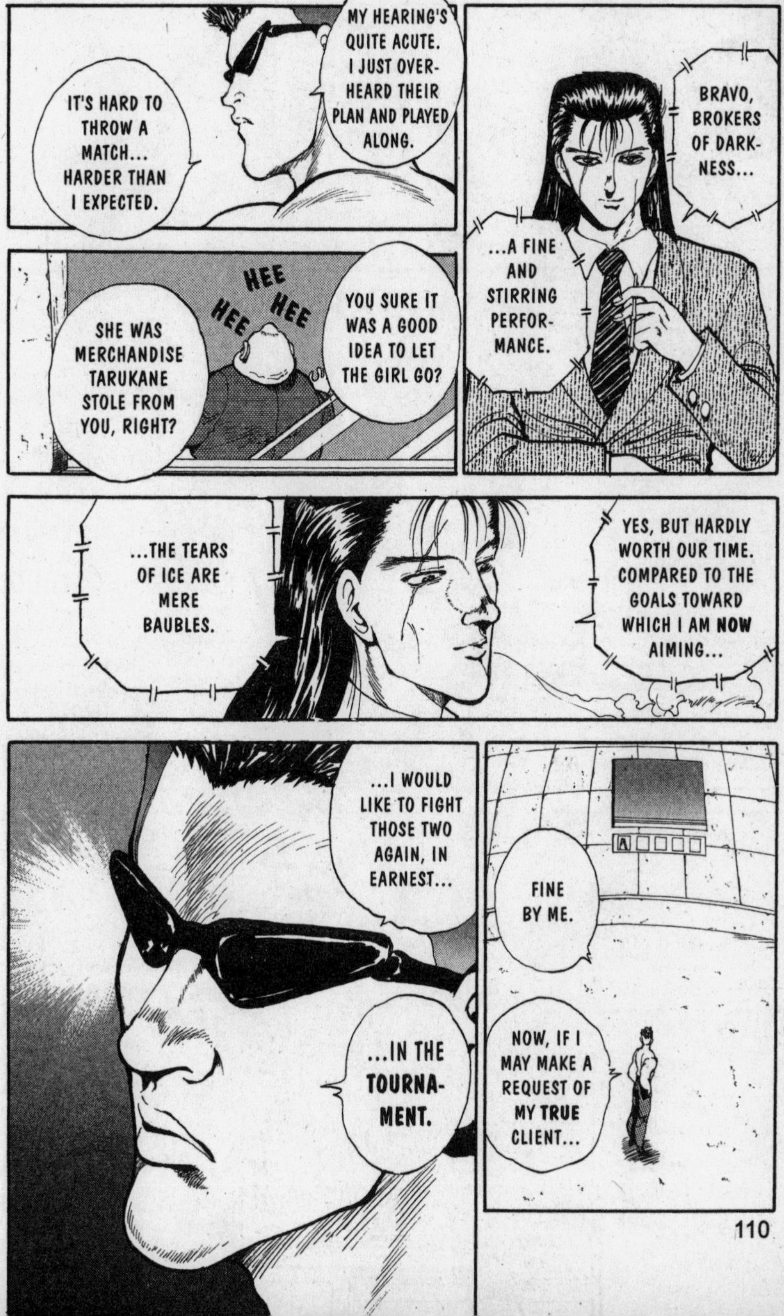
MY HEARING'S QUITE ACUTE. I JUST OVER-HEARD THEIR PLAN AND PLAYED ALONG.
IT'S HARD TO THROW A MATCH... HARDER THAN I EXPECTED.
HEE HEE HEE
YOU SURE IT WAS A GOOD IDEA TO LET THE GIRL GO?
SHE WAS MERCHANDISE TARUKANE STOLE FROM YOU, RIGHT?
BRAVO, BROKERS OF DARK-NESS...
...A FINE AND STIRRING PERFOR-MANCE.
YES, BUT HARDLY WORTH OUR TIME. COMPARED TO THE GOALS TOWARD WHICH I AM NOW AIMING...
...THE TEARS OF ICE ARE MERE BAUBLES.
...I WOULD LIKE TO FIGHT THOSE TWO AGAIN, IN EARNEST...
...IN THE TOURNA-MENT.
FINE BY ME.
NOW, IF I MAY MAKE A REQUEST OF MY TRUE CLIENT...

PRETTY SNEAKY... USING TARUKANE'S DOWNFALL AS A PRETEXT...
...TO WATCH **ME** IN ACTION AGAINST **THEM**.
THEY WILL CERTAINLY BE **INVITED** TO PARTICIPATE.
I'M COUNTING ON THAT.
THE SMALLER ONE... URAMESHI, WHO FIRED THE REIKI BLASTS...
...IS GAINING STRENGTH AT EACH TURN. **HE'LL** BE FORMIDABLE.
SO, HOW DO THEY STACK UP?
HEH HEH... VERY PERCEPTIVE.
WELL, I TRUST YOU'LL MEASURE THE CHALLENGE CAREFULLY. REMEMBER, THE TOURNAMENT IS TWO MONTHS AWAY.
BLIP
OH— BEFORE YOU GO, WOULD YOU MIND TAKING OUT THE TRASH?
AYE AYE, SIR.
...RUINED... MIGHT AS WELL BE DEAD...
...HEE HEE...
...HEE HEE...
TUMP!

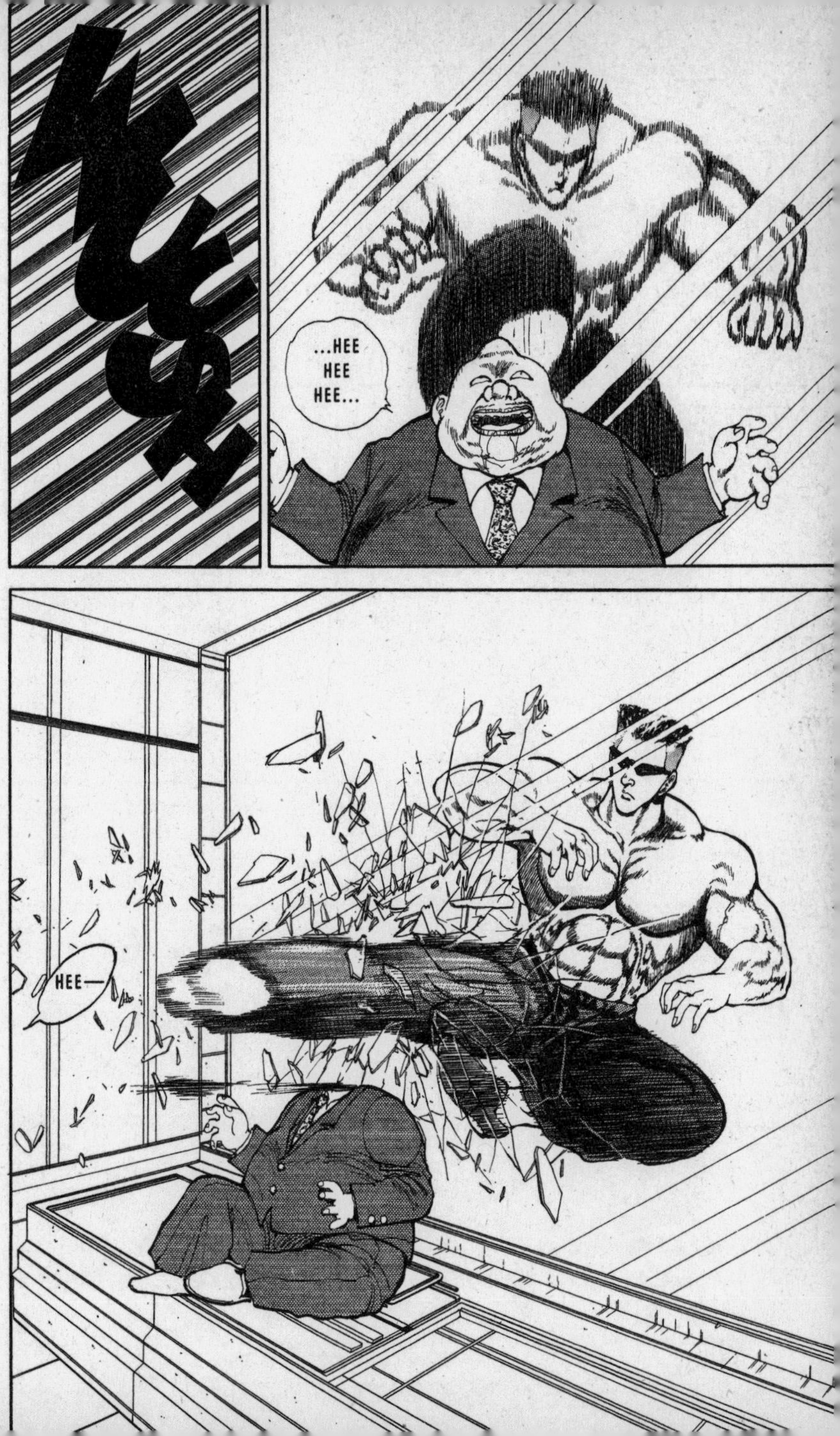
...HEE HEE HEE...
WUSH!
HEE—

I MUST GET STRONGER!!

EIGHT HUNDRED YEN SAYS HE WAS DUMPED!
FOUR HUNDRED YEN SAYS HE SAW A DOWNER MOVIE.
FIVE HUNDRED YEN SAYS IT'S A NEW IMAGE.
AWRIGHT, BETTING'S CLOSED!
HUH? HE WASN'T DUMPED.
KIRI-SHIMA'S PEGGED IT.
WHY D'YA SUPPOSE KUWABARA'S BEEN SO **WOUND UP** LATELY?
YEAH, HE'S SURE BEEN **QUIET** THE PAST COUPLA DAYS.
IN OTHER RESPECTS, THOUGH, THIS CASE LEAVES A BAD AFTER-TASTE.
SNIEF
HIEI COPPED OUT. HE DIDN'T TELL YUKINA HE WAS HER BROTHER...
BUT HIS ICE MAIDEN'S GONE HOME TO THE GLACIERS.
SO? LONG-DISTANCE RELATIONSHIPS CAN BE **VERY ROMANTIC!**
SIGH
HEY, LOSE THE SCHOOLGIRL ACT.

READ THIS WAY

IT'S BEEN A WHILE...
...SINCE I'VE HIT THE PACHINKO PARLORS.
TUP

READ THIS WAY

OUR FIRST ENCOUNTER... WAS NOT ON THE UP-AND-UP.
THANKFULLY, THAT IS OVER AND DONE WITH.
NOW, I'D LIKE TO DISCUSS SOMETHING PERSONAL...
...A SECRET BETWEEN TWO MEN, YOU MIGHT SAY.
YOU GOT A POINT?
GET TO IT!!
HEH...
...YOU SCARED OF ME?

READ THIS WAY
HAH!
DON'T KID YOURSELF!
TOUGH GUY, HUH? WELL...
...YOUR INSTINCTS KNOW OTHERWISE.
IF YOU COULD LEARN ONE THING, LEARN TO RECOGNIZE DANGER.
YOU ARE STRONG...
...AND YOU'LL GET STRONGER.
THAT'S WHY I THOUGHT I'D SHOW YOU...
...THE REAL ME!
BULGE
CRIICK
HAAAAAH!
IT'S ALL ABOUT MUSCLE MASS.
IN OUR FIRST FIGHT, I WAS PROBABLY AT 20%.
...

PHEW...
I'M NOW UP TO ABOUT 60%.
I COULD LEVEL THIS BUILDING IN THREE MINUTES! WANNA SEE?
DOOM
DOOM
DOOM
DOOM

ER...
UH...
.....
IN TWO MONTHS, A **TOURNAMENT** WILL BE HELD.
SWFFT
WEALTHY HUMANS WHO GET THEIR POWER FROM THE DARK WORLD SPONSOR TEAMS OF FIVE DEMONS—THE STRONGEST AND MOST SKILLED.
THE HUMANS DO IT FOR MONEY AND THRILLS... WE **DEMONS** DO IT FOR BLOOD AND PLEASURE.
I EXTEND TO YOU AND KUWABARA AN INVITATION TO COMPETE.
REFUSE, AND I WILL **KILL YOU** RIGHT NOW.
GET IN **SHAPE.** YOUR LIVES DEPEND ON IT...
...AS YOU WILL BE **FIGHTING TO THE DEATH!**

SO WEAK... MY KNEES...
...GIVING WAY... CAN'T MOVE...
NOT GOOD...
NOT GOOD...!!

I SEE BY YOUR FACES...
...THAT YOU'VE RECEIVED YOUR INVITATIONS.
YOU'LL BE ON URAMESHI'S TEAM, OF COURSE.
WHEN YOU SIDE WITH HUMANS...
...IT BRANDS YOU FOREVER.
YOUR FIFTH IS UP TO YOU.
MY ADVICE? SELECT FOR STRENGTH AND SMARTS.
WHAT'RE OUR CHANCES, YOU THINK?
COULDN'T SAY.

WELL, WELL...
...TO WHAT DO I OWE THIS PLEASURE?

SIIIP
I NEED TO BE STRONGER.
MUCH STRONGER. I'VE GOT TWO MONTHS.
HMPH...
FINALLY TAKING THIS SERIOUSLY?
IT AIN'T GONNA BE EASY.

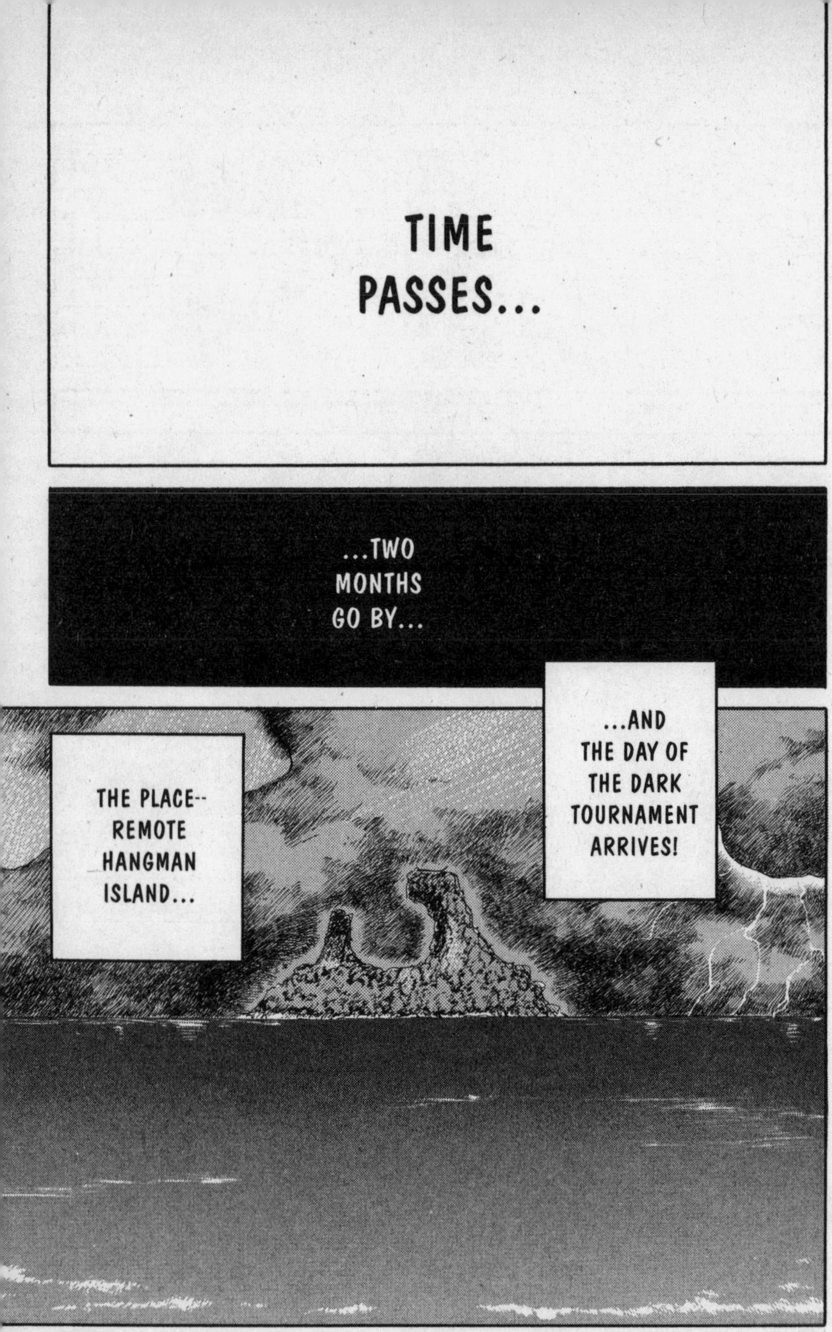
TIME PASSES...
...TWO MONTHS GO BY...
...AND THE DAY OF THE DARK TOURNAMENT ARRIVES!
THE PLACE-- REMOTE HANGMAN ISLAND...

THE DARK
TOURNAMENT
BEGINS!!

THE DARK TOURNAMENT!
FOR UNBRIDLED CLASHES OF EVIL, NOTHING MATCHES THIS CONTEST, HELD BY MORTALS MADE WEALTHY AND POWERFUL THROUGH THE FORCES OF DARKNESS! IN IT, SELECTED FIVE-MEMBER TEAMS BATTLE TO THE DEATH!
REFUSING TO COMPETE MEANS DEATH. THE ONLY WAY TO SURVIVE IS TO WIN.
THOUGH DEMONS ARE THE TYPICAL CONTESTANTS, HUMANS WHO HAVE STUCK THEIR NOSES TOO FAR INTO UNDERWORLD AFFAIRS ARE OFTEN FORCED TO JOIN "GUEST" TEAMS.
GUESTS THIS ROUND ARE:
YUSUKE URAMESHI: HUMAN
KAZUMA KUWABARA: HUMAN
KURAMA: DEMON
IEI: EMON

READ THIS WAY

WHOOB
NIPS

READ THIS WAY

THIS ISN'T STARTING WELL. URAMESHI'S LATE...
...AND WE NEVER ROUNDED UP A FIFTH TEAMMATE.
NEVER MIND ALL THAT. ARE YOU READY?
ME? YOU BETCHA!
KURAMA'S HELPED ME SHAPE UP!
I'M GONNA WIN...
...AND THE DARK WORLD'S GONNA FEAR ME! NO DEMON WILL DARE MESS WITH YUKINA AGAIN!
ALL ABOARD, EVERYBODY. TIME TO GO.
HOLD IT! ONE "GUEST" ISN'T HERE YET!
YEAH? RULES SAY YER LATE, YER A REFUSER.
WE'LL SEND ASSASSINS TO DEAL WITH 'IM.
NO NEED FOR THAT.

READ THIS WAY

.....
YUSUKE.
WHOO! I'M STIFF AND SORE ALL OVER!
YOU LOOK PRETTY SHAKY, AND I HATE TO THINK WHY.
HUP

?
?
SWUFF
SWIFF
SWOOF
WOW!
WHAT STARTED THAT?
THEY'RE MOVING SO...
...SO FAST I ALMOST CAN'T FOLLOW...
PHEW! NICE TO SEE YOU, TOO, HIEI.

I DON'T KNOW HOW YOU DID IT, BUT YOUR SKILLS ARE ALMOST ADEQUATE.
"ALMOST ADEQUATE"? I COULDN'T MOVE LIKE THAT IN A MILLION YEARS!
DON'T SWEAT IT.
YOU DID FOLLOW THEIR MOVES, WHICH SHOWS YOU'VE PRO-GRESSED.
I SUPPOSE SHORT STUFF HERE IS OUR FIFTH MEMBER?
HUH?
SOMEONE SHORTER THAN HIEI?! I CAN BARELY SEE HIM!
IF I SNEEZED I'D BLOW HIM CLEAR TO MARS!
LET'S JUST SAY FOR A FIFTH, WE COULD DO WORSE.
THAT SO? I DUNNO...
IT FILLS THE COUNT. YUSUKE AND I CAN TAKE UP ANY SLACK.
.....

READ THIS WAY

HEY!!
YOW!!
SIXTEEN TEAMS WILL COMPETE IN THE DARK TOURNAMENT! FIFTEEN ARE WAITING ON HANGMAN ISLAND!
ONE TEAM FROM THIS SHIP WILL FILL THE 16TH SLOT!
THAT CIRCULAR DECK ROSE UP!
MUST BE AN ARENA!!
NO ONE TOLD US ABOUT THIS!

EACH TEAM WILL PICK ITS STRONGEST MEMBER...
...AND THESE WILL VIE FOR PARTICIPATION IN THE TOURNAMENT!
A LITTLE WARM-UP MATCH? SUITS ME.
AFTER ALL, WE'RE GONNA WIN.
A BATTLE ROYALE?! IN THOSE IT AIN'T ALWAYS THE STRONGEST WHO COMES OUT ON TOP!
HEY, URAMESHI! HERE'S YOUR CHANCE TO SHOW YOUR NEW STUFF!
YER TEAM CAPTAIN!!
HOW CAN YOU SLEEP?!
C'MON! WAKE UP!
SNORE...
URA-MESHI!!
?!

THIS CAN HAPPEN AFTER EXTREME TRAINING.
HE'S FALLEN INTO DEEP SLEEP TO RESTORE STRENGTH AND AURA.
SAY WHAT?!
THEN WHO'S GOING UP THERE?!
.....
?!
GUESS THAT'S SETTLED. HE'S GOING.
AT LEAST WE'LL GET TO SEE WHAT HE CAN DO.
WHAT IF HE LOSES?!
I DON'T THINK LOSING TEAMS JUST GO HOME!
TUP
PROBABLY RIGHT. WE MIGHT HAVE TO KILL EVERYONE ABOARD...
...SO THERE'LL BE NO ONE LEFT TO COMPLAIN.
TUH-RRIFIC.
RRUMMBLE

BEGIN!
DOOM
HEH HEH... THE PUNY ONE'S FIRST
KILL 'EM IN TURN...
...STARTING WITH YOU!
PILE ON THE SHRIMP!
I KNEW IT! THEY'RE GANGING UP ON HIM!!
NO ROOM TO RUN! HE'LL BE MASHED FLAT!!

SNOOOM

SPLASH!
POINT, GAME, AND MATCH TO TEAM URAMESHI!
THEY WILL TAKE THE 16TH SLOT IN THE DARK TOURNAMENT!
THAT LITTLE GUY USED...
...YU-SUKE'S REIGUN! BUT...
I THINK YU-SUKE...
...KNEW THIS WOULD HAPPEN.
ZZNORK...

THE FIRST OPPONENTS!!

SPLOORSH
HE DEEP-SIXED EVERY ONE O' THEM!
OOOH
USING URAMESHI'S SHOTGUN! WHO IS THAT GUY?!

ADVANCING TO THE 16TH SPOT IN THE TOURNAMENT—
TEAM URAMESHI!!
HUH? WHAT'S—
POINT
.....
JUST ONE THING— WHO ARE YOU?!
THAT WAS ACE! WELCOME TO THE TEAM!!
SCREW THE RULES!
KILL 'EM! WE'LL BE FAMOUS!
ACK!!

YIKES!
RAAAH!
SLICE AND DICE!!
LOOKS LIKE WE'RE UP.
AH WELL, IT'S BETTER THAN SITTING AROUND...
I'D SAY SO...

WUK?
PETAL WHIRL-WIND!!
WOOSH
SPLAT

DOO
!!
HEH! DEAD TO THE WORLD!
AND DEAD FOR REAL IN A SECOND!
AWW, CRIPES! URAMESHI!!
HE'S SO OUT, AKIKO MATSUMOTO COULDN'T STIR HIM IF SHE SANG RIGHT IN HIS EAR!
THAT'S THE LEAST OF YOUR PROBLEMS!
IT'S OVERKILL, BUT...
DOUBLE SWORD FENCING!

CLEAR OFF—
—OR YOU'RE HAMBURGER!!
NO CHANCE!! I'M TAKIN' HIS HEAD...
... AND MAKIN' MY FORTUNE!!
DIE, URAMESHI!!
NO! I'M TOO LATE!!

PRUMP
MNNU-UUH...
...GMMM...
RAAAH! NO WAY, Y'OLD BIDDY!!
I'LL KEEP GOIN' AND GOIN' AND GOIN'!
WHEW! EVEN IN HIS SLEEP, HE TRAINS!
THE REGIMEN'S BECOME INSTINCT-IVE!
OLD BIDDY?!
SO HE WAS TRAINING WITH...
...THAT SHRIMP-BOAT OF A SENSEI...
...MASTER GENKAI?!

READ THIS WAY
FWIT
YAAH!!
BAM
POW
HRAASH
COULDN'T BE HER! WHY'D SHE RISK HER NECK?
RAARGH
IF NOT HER, THEN WHO...?
HMM...
WHAP
CRACK
MR. SAKYO WAS RIGHT... RANDOM THUGS JUST ANNOY THESE GUYS.
I'D HOPED TO SEE THEIR POTENTIAL, BUT THEY'RE BARELY GIVING 10%.

WEEEOOOO
THAT'S GOTTA BE HANGMAN ISLAND!!
WHO KNOWS WHAT HORRORS AWAIT US THERE?!
BRACE YERSELVES, GUYS!! AND LOOK SHARP!!

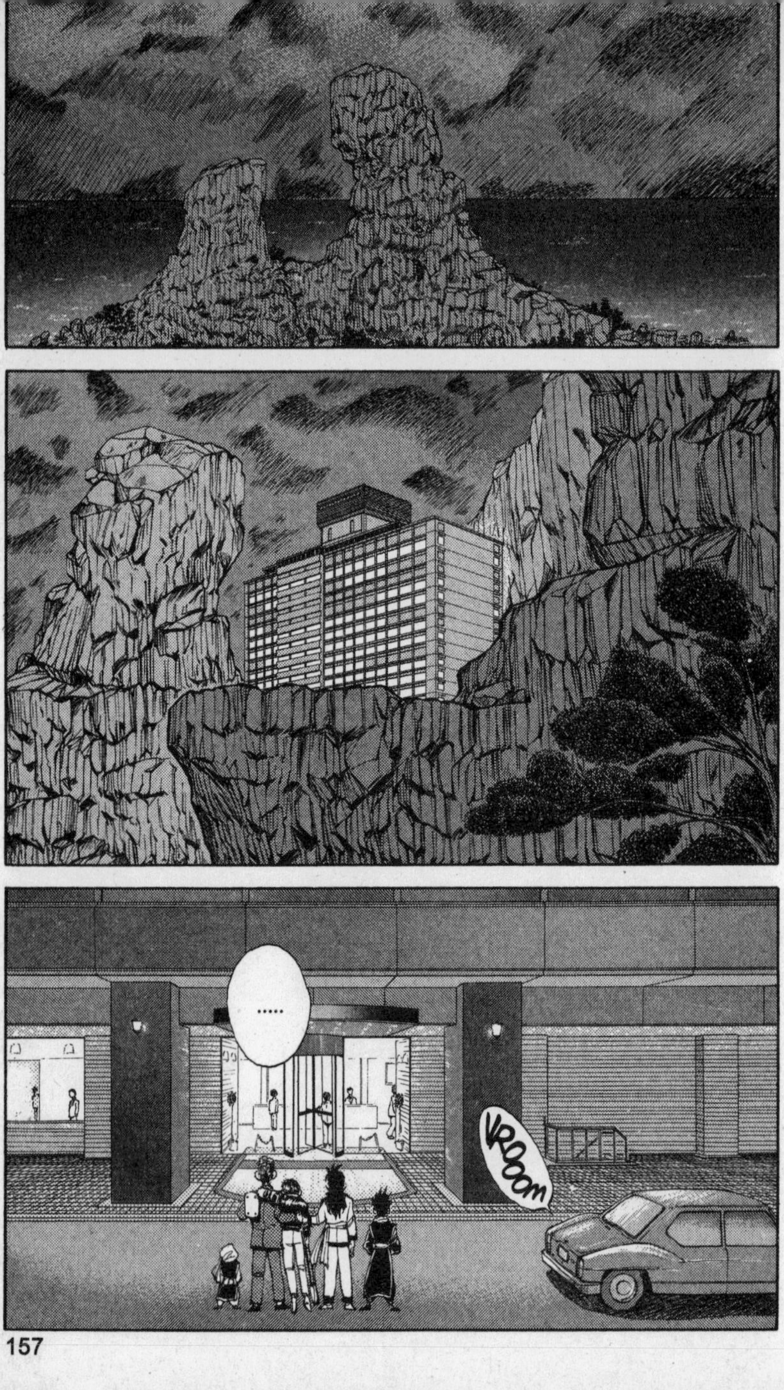
......
VROOOM

GEEZ...
...PRETTY **RITZY JOINT.** WHAT GIVES?
YOWZA
WELCOME, HONORED GUESTS.
LET ME SHOW YOU TO YOUR ROOM.
TAMURA
BONANZA WEIRD. **THIS** IS THE DARK TOURNAMENT?
SNOZZ...
HEH HEH
THERE GO THE SACRIFICIAL LAMBS...
HEH HEH
AH... SO YOUNG AND UNSUSPECTING...
SO WHERE **IS** HE, BOTAN? HUH?!
CALM DOWN, KEIKO.
TUMP
ZZZ...

HOW CAN I CALM DOWN?! WE ALMOST DIED BECAUSE OF YUSUKE!
WE HAVE TO KEEP TRACK OF WHERE HE GOES, WHAT HE DOES, SO WE CAN BE READY—
I'LL WHUP HIM!
NOT SO LOUD!
I KNOW, I KNOW.
GROWING UP WITH YUSUKE, SHE HAD TO BE PLUCKY AND FEARLESS!
SHE DIDN'T BLINK WHEN I TOLD HER ABOUT THE TOURNAMENT— SHE JUST SNARLED, "TAKE ME THERE!"
NEXT EPISODE: HOW THEY MANAGED IT!
WOW! SHIZUKA, CHECK OUT THAT CHANDELIER!
I'M WOR-RIED...
404
MAN, TALK ABOUT POSH!
THIS'D BE A GREAT VACATION SPOT!!

GENTLE-MEN...
GLARE...
THIS STUFF AIN'T POISONED, IS IT?
NOT LIKELY. THE TOURNAMENT'S ALL ABOUT MAXIMUM COMBAT, SO THEY WANT EVERY CONTENDER AT PEAK POTENTIAL.
THE HOSTS ARE ESPECIALLY INTERESTED IN SEEING US IN ACTION BEFORE WE'RE TORN LIMB BY LIMB...
WELL, IT NEVER HURTS TO BE CAREFUL.
I'LL STICK TO MY OWN BEVERAGES, THANKS.
DOOOM
Energy Drink
Pierre Taki
?!
ODD... THERE'S A CUP MISSING.
HUH? THERE'S FIVE OF US, AND FIVE CUPS.
I HAVEN'T TAKEN ONE, SO...

READ THIS WAY

HEH HEH...
BARUM
HEY!!
WHO'S THAT?! HOW'D HE GET IN HERE?!
HE MUST'VE BEEN HIDING SOMEPLACE!
THEN CAME OUT AND TOOK THE CUP WITHOUT US NOTICING...
NAW, I CAME THROUGH THE DOOR, LIKE YOU DID!
FORGOT TO KNOCK, THOUGH.
ALLOW ME TO INTRODUCE MYSELF— RINKU, TEAM SPECIAL OPS.
MY CREW, THE JOLLY DEVIL SIX, WILL BE YOUR OPPONENTS IN THE FIRST ROUND TOMORROW.
NOD
"JOLLY DEVIL SIX"?
ISN'T IT ONLY FIVE TO A TEAM?!

YOU DIDN'T KNOW YOU COULD BRING A BACKUP IN CASE ONE OF YOU DIES IN BATTLE?
THE SIX OF US ARE ALL TOUGH AS NAILS, SO WE CHOSE OUR ALTERNATE BY ROCK-PAPER-SCISSORS.
MUST BE NICE BEING THE GUEST TEAM. YOU DON'T HAVE TO SIT THROUGH OPENING CERE-MONIES OR RULE MEETINGS.
'COURSE, YOU ALSO DON'T NEED TO NEGOTIATE FOR PRIZES 'CUZ YOU'LL BE TAKEN OUT WAY EARLY.
LI'L PUNK THINKS HE'S BEIN' FUNNY?
I'LL SHOW HIM FUNNY IF HE KEEPS THIS UP.
IT'S JUST A FACT. THE CAPTAIN OF THE PREVIOUS WINNING TEAM NOMINATED YOU GUYS AS GUESTS...
... BUT FROM WHAT I SEE, I COULD TAKE Y'ALL MYSELF IN AN ELIMINATION MATCH (WHERE IF ONE MEMBER BEATS ANOTHER, HE KEEPS GOING TO FIGHT THE NEXT PERSON AND THE NEXT, UNTIL HE LOSES. THEN THEY SWITCH TO THEIR SECOND MEMBER, ETC.)
THAT WILL DO, RINKU...

DOOM
DOOM
DOOM
ANOTHER LURKER!!
HE WASN'T THERE BEFORE, I'M SURE OF IT!!
SLIPPED BY ME, TOO!
SORRY, ZERU! GOT CARRIED AWAY!
THIS TOURNAMENT STUFF IS JUST SO EXCITING!

READ THIS WAY

THE VANGUARD BATTLE BEGINS!!

I DECLARE THE DARK TOURNAMENT OFFICIALLY UNDERWAY!!!
THE ORDINARY, LAW-ABIDING CITIZENS OF THE WORLD WILL NEVER KNOW THE THRILL OF WATCHING HELL UNLEASHED.
HEH HEH HEH... THIS IS THE BEST PART OF SELLING ONE'S SOUL TO THE DARK SIDE.
VIP SEATS

THE VANGUARD BATTLE BEGINS!!
PUBLIC SEATS
WE WANT HITTING, KICKING, POKES IN THE EYE!
WE DIDN'T DO ANY OF THAT FOR WEEKS SO WE COULD BE HERE!
THE RULES BAR THOSE WHO DO BAD DEEDS! SO LET'S SEE SOME!!

DOON
WOW, CHECK OUT THAT CROWD!
IT'S THE JOLLY DEVIL SIX— SCRAPPY STARS OF THE SLUMS!!
SHUFF
RAAAH
RAAAH
RAAAH
THEY'RE THE REAL CHALLENGE TO YOUR TEAM TOGURO.
URAMESHI'S TEAM WILL BE DISPATCHED, IN SHORT.
WHAT DO YOU THINK, MR. SAKYO? THEY'RE JUST DREGS OF THE RED-LIGHT DISTRICT...
... BUT THEY HAVE POTENTIAL. LEGENDS IN THE MAKING, I BELIEVE.
JOLLY DEVIL SIX'S SPONSOR: MEMBER OF THE BBC, SUKEZO GONDAWARA

THE "GUESTS" HAVE ARRIVED!
LOOK! URAMESHI'S ALREADY FAINTED!
TRAITORS! HOPE THEY CHEW YOU UP AND SPIT YOU OUT!
NO WAY YOU'RE COMIN' OUT ALIVE!
HIEI! KURAMA! HUMAN-LOVIN' BASTARDS!
HISS
BOO
TEAMS TO THE CENTER, PLEASE!!
SHUK
CALLING US TRAITORS? IF THEY WEREN'T SUCH LOWLIFES, I'D TAKE OFFENSE.
FRIENDLY BUNCH...
...GUESS THEY HAVE TO VENT ON SOMEBODY.

KOENMA JR.--HUMAN WORLD VERSION

THE LAW IS DECIDED BY THE VICTOR...
...AND EVEN YOU HOLD NO RANK OVER ANY OTHER SPECTATOR. YOU COULD NOT OBJECT IF YOU SAW YOUR OWN PARENTS MURDERED.
MASTER KOENMA! YUSUKE'S TEAM'S IN THE ARENA!!
GOT IT. THANKS.
WOW! SOME HAREM!
YOU'RE QUITE THE LADIES MAN, SIR!
FRIENDS AND FAMILY OF THE "GUESTS."
ONCE MY LOOSE-LIPPED SUB-ORDINATE WAS THROUGH, I HAD TO BRING THEM ALONG.
I WAS JUST TRYING TO BE NICE!
HMM... WELL...
...THREE HUMAN WOMEN BOLD ENOUGH TO COME HERE.

PULP TH' SCUM!
RAAH
RAAH
RIP 'EM APART!!
RAAH
POUND 'EM TO JELLY!!
SNOORE...
STILL ASLEEP.
THE TEAM CAPTAINS WILL DECIDE THE MODE OF BATTLE AND WHAT CONSTITUTES A WIN.
IF THEY'RE UNABLE TO AGREE, HOUSE RULES STIPULATE EACH MEMBER FIGHT ONE-ON-ONE. THE TEAM WITH THE MOST VICTORIES TAKES THE MATCH.
THE CAP-TAIN...?
YUSUKE'S STILL OUT.
THEN IT'S YOUR OFFICE, KUWABARA.

Y'MEAN ME?
SAY WHAT?
SHEE...
STOMP
STOMP
I'LL SHOW 'EM LEADERSHIP!
IT MEANS BEING URA-MESHI'S SECOND, BUT WHAT THE HECK?!
SHUCKS, I'M FLATTERED!
NOT THAT IT MATTERS, BUT I'M FOR ONE-ON-ONE.
IT PROLONGS THE FUN.
IT'S A REAL MAN'S WAY TO FIGHT!!
SOUNDS GOOD TO ME!

ZZZ
IT'S BEEN DECIDED--FIVE ONE-ON-ONE BATTLES!
SIGH
WAZZAT COOL OR WOT?
IT'S OBVIOUS HE'S TRYING TO PROVOKE YUSUKE!
CRIPES! HIS AURA'S HOT AS AN OVEN!!
HE'S OUT TO KILL...
!!
ICY EYES AND A FIERY AURA... YET ZERU HANGS OUT IN THE HUMAN WORLD? WHAT'S DEMONKIND COME TO...?

READ THIS WAY

ALL THAT TEASING YESTERDAY DIDN'T SCARE HIM.
SIGH... I ALWAYS GET THE DOOFUSES.
BRAIN-DEAD, FOR SURE.
A COUNT OF 10 WILL DETERMINE OUT-OF-BOUNDS AND KNOCKDOWNS.
IN ONE-ON-ONE, THE RULES ARE— ANYTHING GOES!!
BOOOOO
KUWA-BARA'S UP! BLEAH!
KILL HIM!!
KWANG
BEGIN!!
WELL, HERE GOES.
YOU GOT IT!!
PWANG!!
OKAY, SHRIMP, BRING IT!!

READ THIS WAY
WHOA!
RINKU DISPLAYS AMAZING AGILITY! I, KOTO, YOUR COMMENTATOR, CAN BARELY FOLLOW HIM!
THAT'LL DO!
HE CAN'T SEE ME...
!!

WHAM
!!
THE GLOVES ARE OFF, KID!!
WHAT...?
DIDYA SEE THAT?
UNREAL!!

READ THIS WAY

HUCK...
HE'S GOT HIM!
THIS IS IT!!
WHSH

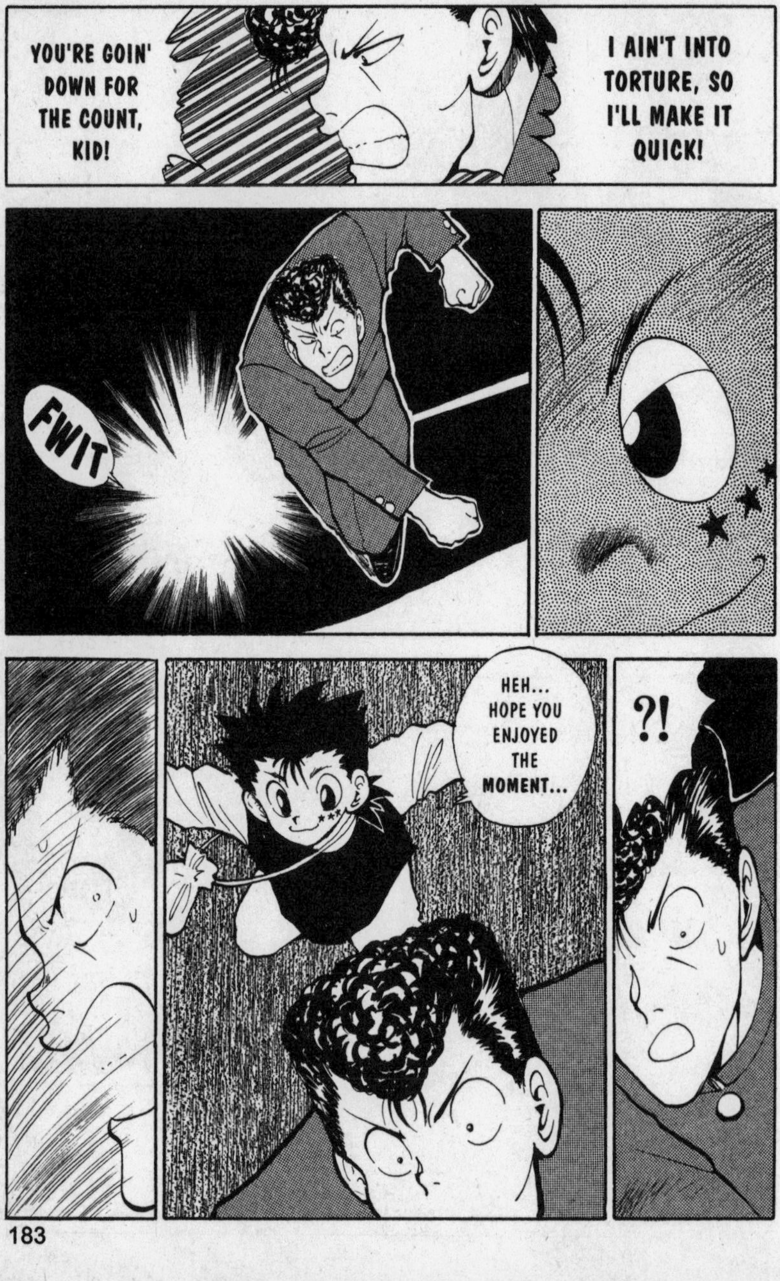
I AIN'T INTO TORTURE, SO I'LL MAKE IT QUICK!
YOU'RE GOIN' DOWN FOR THE COUNT, KID!
FWIT
?!
HEH... HOPE YOU ENJOYED THE MOMENT...

KWACK
1!
...'CAUSE THE MOMENT'S OVER! HA HA HA!
2!
OOO!
I COULDA POPPED HIM RIGHT OFF, BUT WHERE'S THE FUN IN THAT?

I SNAPPED HIS NECK.
DON'T BOTHER COUNTING. HE'S DEAD.
RAAAH RAAAH
MIGHTY FINE, THAT!
SUPER AWESOME, LI'L DUDE!
THAT LITTLE GREASE BALL...
...ENJOYS A FIGHT TOO, I'D SAY.
...YOU BROKE MY NECK?
SO YOU SAY...
!!
HE BEAT THE COUNT! THE BATTLE WILL RESUME!!
CRICK
.....
THEN I'LL HAVE TO RETURN THE FAVOR... IN SPADES!

OOOOOH
TOUGH SONUVAGUN—STILL STANDING AFTER THAT KICK!
FINISH IT, RUNT!! KILL HIM!
THE SECRET OF DEVIL YO-YOS!!
RINKU USES PSYCHOLOGICAL TACTICS TO CATCH THE OTHER OFF-GUARD, AND KUWABARA TAKES IT IN STRIDE!!
IT'S ONLY THE FIRST MATCH OF THE TOURNAMENT, BUT THE TENSION IS ALREADY PALPABLE!
GOTTA SAY, HE OUTWITTED ME...
...BUT THAT KICK TO MY HEAD DIDN'T DO ME IN...
...SO HE AIN'T MUCH TO WORRY ABOUT.
.....

THE SECRET OF DEVIL YO-YOS!!

NOW I GET WHY YOU WERE INVITED AS "GUESTS."
YOU WITHSTOOD MY DIRECT ATTACK, SO I'LL BRING OUT MY...
...DEMONIC TRICKS.
DEVIL YO-YOS!!!
SERIOUS PLAYTIME, EH?

BATTER UP, PAL!!
SHOT!
SPRING!
!!
I'LL JUST SPLIT 'EM...
HMPH! SIMPLE!
SHOOM

WHAT...?!
WHOP
THOSE YOYOS ZIGZAG LIKE SNAKES!
WHAT A STYLISH MOVE!
OOOOH
RINKU'S YO-YOS FAKED OUT KUWABARA'S BUTT GOOD!

HEY, MORON...
...DIDYA THINK I WAS JUST GONNA PLAY AROUND?
Whirrr
MY AURA GOES RIGHT FROM MY FINGERS TO THE YO-YOS...
...EACH OF WHICH I CONTROL INDIVIDUALLY.
HISSS
LIKE SO!
OH BOY...!

YOUR DULL OL' AURA SWORDS WON'T EVEN CUT THE STRINGS!!
FWASH
THEY'RE SLICIN' UP THE GROUND AS THEY GO!
VOOOSH
YOICKS!!

SKREEE
BLAST!!
WZZRRR
WHAM
HE MAY BE SMALL, BUT HIS YO-YOS KICK BUTT.
RINKU'S POWERS WORK BEST THROUGH WEAPONS.
THEY GO WHEREVER HE WILLS!

?!
TWIRL
TWIRL
WHUP
WHAT?!
THOSE YO-YOS HAVE LIFTED KUWABARA'S BODY INTO THE AIR!!
ROUND THE WORLD!!
WHOA!
URF!!
WOOSH

WHIP 'IM 'ROUND AGAIN!!
BLOOD! WE WANT BLOOD!!
.....
RAAH
RAAH
CAN'T SAY MUCH FOR YOUR COACH-ING, KURAMA. YOUR STUDENT'S BEEN LAID OUT FLAT.
GURF!
WHAM
DRAT-TED...
AGH...
I ADMIT...
...WE HAVEN'T SEEN MUCH YET.

YOU'RE A TOUGH ONE TO FINISH OFF.
AND THIS IS JUST THE FIRST DAY. BETTER WRAP THIS UP.
...PUNK!
I'LL KILL YOU...!!
RAAH
HEY, THE TOURNAMENT'S STARTED ALREADY!!
RAAH
THEY'RE CHEERING LIKE MAD! WHO'S WINNING?
OH, NO! LOOK!!
KUWA-BARA!
THAT KID'S GOT HIM SOARING LIKE A KITE!!

READ THIS WAY

THAT'S YUSUKE'S MOM: CLUELESS

KUWABARA'S SISTER—
POWERFUL SIXTH SENSE, THERE.

THAT SHOULD DO IT.
DROP HIM! KILL HIM!
LEMME DOWN!
YER DEAD NOW, HUMAN!
YOU'LL GO SPLAT—LIKE AN EGG!
WHIIIRR
HE'S FALLING!!
RAAAH!
SHOOM
THIS IS THE END!

SWORD, GROW!!
KA-ZZZAK
NOT YET, IT AIN'T!
!!
HARF!
ZREEEK
HE PLUNGED HIS SWORD INTO THE GROUND TO BREAK HIS FALL AND—
THUNK!!
—FLING HIM FOR-WARD!!

SWEET MOVE, GUY.
YOU'RE DARN CLEVER IN A PINCH.
BUT NOW...
...YOUR TRAJECTORY IS...
...SENDING YOU STRAIGHT AT ME!
AND THAT JUST BEGS FOR A SALVO OF YO-YOS RIGHT IN YOUR FACE!!
WHOOSH
YOU FORGOT!!
I'VE GOT A SECOND SWORD!!
SO WHAT?
A STRAIGHT SWORD'S EASY TO DODGE—
SHUP

ZWANG
ZWING
ZOING
WHAT...?!
IT'S THREADING THROUGH THE YO-YO STRINGS?!

READ THIS WAY

UH... OH...
G-GOTCHA...!
NICE.
THEY KNOCKED EACH OTHER OUT COLD—
OOOO
—AND OUT OF BOUNDS!!

Sigh...

I can't think of anything...

There goes that idea.

IN THE NEXT VOLUME...

Survival becomes the ultimate goal as Team Urameshi suffers the gut-wrenching agony of competition at Hangman Island's Dark Tournament. Kurama tackles Roto of Jolly Devil Six and is caught off-guard by his wily opponent's nefarious tactics. Witness Kurama's combat expertise when sinister Roto leans heavily on his most vulnerable spot.

Coming June 2005

VIZ
PRINCESS SIENNA
LEADS THE ATTACK ON
SANCTUARY!
Only
$7.95
Each
Vol.1-8
On Sale Now!
SAINT ★ SEIYA
KNIGHTS
OF THE
ZODIAC™
ON SALE AT:
www.shonenjump.com
Also available at your local
bookstore, comic store and
Suncoast Motion Picture Company.
COMIC SHOP LOCATOR SERVICE
888-COMIC-BOOK
888-266-4226
SHONEN JUMP
GRAPHIC NOVELS
SAINT SEIYA © 1986 by MASAMI KURUMADA/SHUEISHA Inc.
Covers subject to change.

LUFFY AND HIS CREW
CATCH BLACK CAT FEVER!
Only $7.95 Each!
Volumes 1-5 on Sale Now!
ONE PIECE
Now Airing on the FoxBox!
SHONEN JUMP GRAPHIC NOVELS
On Sale At:
www.shonenjump.com
Also available at your local bookstore, comic store and Suncoast Motion Picture Company.
ONE PIECE © 1997 by EIICHIRO ODA / SHUEISHA Inc. Covers subject to change.

SUBSCRIBE TODAY & BECOME A
MEMBER OF THE SHONEN JUMP
SUBSCRIBER CLUB...
You'll get:
*Access to Exclusive Online Content!
*50% Savings Off the Newsstand Price!
*Exclusive Prizes!
All this available ONLY to Subscribers!
SHONEN JUMP
THE WORLD'S MOST POPULAR MANGA TM
FILL OUT THE SUBSCRIPTION CARD ON THE OTHER SIDE, OR SUBSCRIBE ONLINE AT:
www.shonenjump.com

COMPLETE OUR SURVEY AND LET US KNOW WHAT YOU THINK!

☐ Please do NOT send me information about VIZ and SHONEN JUMP products, news and events, special offers, or other information.

☐ Please do NOT send me information from VIZ's trusted business partners.

Name: ______________________________

Address: ______________________________

City: ______________ **State:** ______ **Zip:** ______________

E-mail: ______________________________

☐ **Male** ☐ **Female** **Date of Birth** (mm/dd/yyyy): ___/___/______ (**Under 13? Parental consent required**)

1 Do you purchase SHONEN JUMP Magazine?

☐ Yes ☐ No **(if no, skip the next two questions)**

If **YES**, do you subscribe?

☐ Yes ☐ No

If **NO**, how often do you purchase SHONEN JUMP Magazine?

☐ 1-3 issues a year

☐ 4-6 issues a year

☐ more than 7 issues a year

2 Which SHONEN JUMP Graphic Novel did you purchase? **(please check one)**

☐ Beet the Vandel Buster ☐ Bleach ☐ Dragon Ball

☐ Dragon Ball Z ☐ Hikaru no Go ☐ Knights of the Zodiac

☐ Naruto ☐ One Piece ☐ Rurouni Kenshin

☐ Shaman King ☐ The Prince of Tennis ☐ Ultimate Muscle

☐ Whistle! ☐ Yu-Gi-Oh! ☐ YuYu Hakusho

☐ Other ______________________

Will you purchase subsequent volumes?

☐ Yes ☐ No

3 How did you learn about this title? **(check all that apply)**

☐ Favorite title ☐ Advertisement ☐ Article

☐ Gift ☐ Read excerpt in SHONEN JUMP Magazine

☐ Recommendation ☐ Special offer ☐ Through TV animation

☐ Website ☐ Other ______________________

4 Of the titles that are serialized in SHONEN JUMP Magazine, have you purchased the Graphic Novels?

☐ Yes ☐ No

If **YES**, which ones have you purchased? (check all that apply)

☐ Dragon Ball Z ☐ Hikaru no Go ☐ Naruto ☐ One Piece
☐ Shaman King ☐ Yu-Gi-Oh! ☐ YuYu Hakusho

If **YES**, what were your reasons for purchasing? (please pick up to 3)

☐ A favorite title ☐ A favorite creator/artist ☐ I want to read it in one go
☐ I want to read it over and over again ☐ There are extras that aren't in the magazine
☐ The quality of printing is better than the magazine ☐ Recommendation
☐ Special offer ☐ Other

If **NO**, why did/would you not purchase it?

☐ I'm happy just reading it in the magazine ☐ It's not worth buying the graphic novel
☐ All the manga pages are in black and white unlike the magazine
☐ There are other graphic novels that I prefer ☐ There are too many to collect for each title
☐ It's too small ☐ Other ______

5 Of the titles NOT serialized in the Magazine, which ones have you purchased?
(check all that apply)

☐ Beet the Vandel Buster ☐ Bleach ☐ Dragon Ball
☐ Knights of the Zodiac ☐ The Prince of Tennis ☐ Rurouni Kenshin
☐ Whistle! ☐ Other ______ ☐ None

If you did purchase any of the above, what were your reasons for purchase?

☐ A favorite title ☐ A favorite creator/artist
☐ Read a preview in SHONEN JUMP Magazine and wanted to read the rest of the story
☐ Recommendation ☐ Other

Will you purchase subsequent volumes?

☐ Yes ☐ No

6 What race/ethnicity do you consider yourself? (please check one)

☐ Asian/Pacific Islander ☐ Black/African American ☐ Hispanic/Latino
☐ Native American/Alaskan Native ☐ White/Caucasian ☐ Other

THANK YOU! Please send the completed form to: VIZ Survey
42 Catharine St.
Poughkeepsie, NY 12601

All information provided will be used for internal purposes only. We promise not to sell or otherwise divulge your information.